Commendation for *The Generous Soul*

So far, planet Earth has seen the rise of one and only one fantastically wealthy nation—the United States of America. But increasingly we who plumb the depths of this swirling sea of money and privilege and convenience are confronting what James Houston aptly identifies as the failure of success. In *The Generous Soul* Marty Duren compels a confrontation between the affluent society and the generosity-shaped activity and purposes of God. In clear, accessible, penetrating prose, Duren reminds us or perhaps teaches us for the first time that hands clinched tight around the American dream are neither free to embrace Jesus nor to enjoy the benefits purchased for sinners on the Cross and woven into the very gospel itself.

Dr. Mark DeVine, Associate Professor of History and Doctrine, Beeson Divinity School, Samford University and author of *Bonhoeffer Speaks Today: Following Jesus at All Costs*

Marty Duren has written a very helpful book that challenges the apathetic giving patterns of American Christians. The reason that so many give so little is not a matter of economics but of spirituality and biblical literacy (or, more accurately, illiteracy). The Bible clearly teaches what Marty calls "missional giving" and when Christians embrace the call of God to be "missionary managers" of His resources then the church will be filled with "generous souls." Read this book to be challenged to think rightly about and handle responsibly whatever amount of wealth God has entrusted to you.

Dr. Tom Ascol, Pastor
Grace Baptist Church, Cape Coral, Florida

This is a hard-hitting, take-no-prisoners rendition of biblical stewardship that gets at the heart of Jesus' take and example on material possessions. A missional style of living/giving is not an option for any Jesus follower, it is a joyful mandate, as Duren makes indelibly clear and convincing. His personable writing style interlaced with his own life experience plus appropriate items from pop culture make his work an interesting read. His exegetical rigor with the biblical sources and his prophetic challenge hit squarely the open nerve of materialism that inundates so much of Christian living today. I highly recommend it!

Dr. Jimmy Cobb, Professor of Christian Theology, History and Ethics
Canadian Southern Baptist Seminary & College

Great books are written by people who have experience, and heart knowledge of the subject about which they are writing. I've watched, learned and been influenced by Marty in the last 20 years as God gave

much of this heart knowledge to him. This book has something for all whether the experienced faithful servant, Bible teacher, new believer or struggling Christian. Read it and allow God to energize your faith to give missionally.
Joe Wilson, Europe/Asia Church Planter, Baptist International Mission Agency
Novosibirsk, Siberia, Russia

Like most pastors, with very busy schedules and an endless supply of matters requiring attention, I thought I would read The Generous Soul in small pieces as I found time. Wow! I could not put it down. I quickly found myself pushing other things aside so that I could keep reading. This is not just another stewardship book. The Biblical truths, the stories, the ideas behind missional giving, were all gripping. Throughout my time in the book, I found myself being challenged, encouraged, inspired and convicted. The Generous Soul is a must read for anyone who wants to honor God with their resources, and advance those things that are near to His heart.
Jeff Sellers, Pastor
Victory Church @ Lakeside Village, Lakeland, FL

It's been said that Satan's two major weapons to slow down the gospel are persecution and prosperity. A stroll through most church parking lots on Sunday morning will quickly point to which is being used in America. *The Generous Soul* by Marty Duren is written with a wit and conviction that sheds light on a billion dollar blind spot. We have not only bought into the American dream, but we have called it Christian. *The Generous Soul* calls us back to a sacrificial life-style that is Christ-like, yet counter-cultural for most church attendees with encouragement for all those who desire to live each day in a manner that reflects God's missional heart.
Keith Keller, Director for Expedition 237
United World Mission

The Generous Soul is captivating and convicting; at times humorous, but always courageous. Those who read it will be better for it as they are taken into a new dimension of what it means to be missional. Marty has been in my inner circle of friends for almost 25 years. I know him well. I love him dearly. I admire him greatly. He writes this book with integrity and ease, because he is a generous soul!
Todd Wright, Lead Pastor, Midway Church, Villa Rica, GA and co-author of *JOURNEYS: Transitioning Churches to Relevance*

The Generous Soul takes a fresh and compelling look at our responsibility as stewards of God's resources. As Duren states, 'Spending the money God has entrusted to our management, without

His involvement, is embezzlement.' This book will challenge you to the core.
Kiki Cherry, New Life Campus Ministry
Carnegie Mellon University

For most of my life I had this notion that there was my Church life where I prayed and listened to sermons and sang. And then there was my real life where I made money, bought a house, amassed possessions that allowed me to keep up with the American Dream. Marty Duren smashes that notion with the statement, "Our use of money is not a separate reality from the gospel." Marty has written a book that I hope finds its way into the hands of the believers that populate our churches and the Pastors who lead them. What he postulates is truth that we not only need to hear, but we need to put in practice.
Darren Tyler, Lead Pastor
Conduit Church, Franklin, TN

Marty Duren joins the growing number of Christ followers who recognize that something is dreadfully wrong in our current system of Christian economic activity. He issues a challenge to take seriously the call to missional engagement and embrace a lifestyle of generosity that shows the true beauty of what Kingdom living is all about. Theologically astute and rich in stories of remarkable giving and receiving, *The Generous Soul* will guide the reader toward a better sense of what it means to truly give "all" to Christ our Lord.
John Elam, Director of Missions
Northwestern Baptist Association, Woodward, OK

After reading this book, I am left with an overwhelming desire to pass this 'test of faithfulness' and be seen in God's eyes as a 'generous soul.' When I walk the dirt paths of Africa, the need for and the lack of missional giving is painfully evident. If we truly believe that God is the owner and sustainer of all things, we will not only obey His commission to go, but we will also surrender our lives to give. Marty has rightly divided God's Word to reveal that any spiritual investment offered now will pale in comparison to the eternal inheritance that awaits.
Beth Holt, Heavenbound Ministries, Millerville, AL and author of *It is Well*

Stewardship has fallen on hard times. Competing with the wider consumerist culture, pastors struggle to find helpful material on giving. Denominational material is often over-simplified. Financial programs are more 'how-to' than 'what-for.' In *The Generous Soul*, Marty Duren offers a theology of missional giving - that is, giving located squarely in

the context of God and His Kingdom. We plan to use *The Generous Soul* at Snow Hill in small groups and recommended reading for those interesting in a theology of giving.
Todd Littleton, Pastor
Snow Hill Baptist Church, Tuttle, OK

The Generous Soul tells it like it is: most of us have a problem with materialism - it has even entrenched itself big time into our Christianity. But Duren doesn't just condemn us for our devotion to things; he gives us help and Biblical insight in our ongoing struggle in dethroning the god of mammon. Aided by a fresh biblical perspective and stories from his own journey, we get a glimpse into what life would be like if we were to become generous souls.
David Brazzeal, Composer, Writer, Chaplain to the Arts
Paris, France

I started my review of *The Generous Soul* by reading it as I would read any book. It was, after all, just another item on my "to do" list. But then, I noticed that something happened. It would not permit me to read it from a detached perspective. Each chapter prompted me to reflect on, and wrestle with, the hold that money and possessions have on my soul. The reader will especially resonate with Marty's personal stories of God's faithfulness and timely provisions. Prepare to be challenged!
Dr. Gary Elkins, Professor of Philosophy
Toccoa Falls College

Wow! What a remarkable challenge and reminder. In a sea of Christian literature, this is a book every professing believer needs to read. But make no mistake, it is not for the faint of heart. Quite simply, it is a call to put your actions and monies where Jesus' heart is - on seeking, serving, and saving the lost. In my opinion, Marty has cut to the chase and has driven a stake through the heart of en vogue "missional" living that has pierced both my conscience and my wallet.
Dr. Joey Rodgers, Financial Planner
Catalyst Wealth Services

The Generous Soul takes a refreshing and holistic look at the church's response to God's ownership, painting a compelling picture of what the life of a Christ follower should look like. In the midst of these uncertain economic times, this is a must-read for pastors and church-goers alike.
Jason Berry, Campus Pastor
12Stone Church, Flowery Branch, GA

THE GENEROUS SOUL

AN INTRODUCTION TO MISSIONAL GIVING

MARTY DUREN

MISSIONAL PRESS

Published by Missional Press
149 Golden Plover Court
Smyrna, DE 19977
www.missional-press.com
twitter.com/missionalpress

Printed in the United States of America.

Author photo credit: Abigail Duren
Cover design: Sam Raynor
Piggy bank image: dreamstime.com

Scriptures noted with NKJV are from the New King James Version of the Holy Bible, Copyright © 1979, 1980, 1982, 1988, Thomas Nelson, Inc.; ESV are from The Holy Bible, English Standard Version, Copyright © 2001 by Crossway Bibles, a division of Good News Publishers; NASB are from the New American Standard Bible®, Copyright © 1960, 1962, 1963, 1968, 1971, 1972, 1973, 1975, 1977, 1995, by the Lockman Foundation; NIV are from the Holy Bible, New International Version, Copyright © 1973, 1978, 1984, International Bible Society; HCSB are from the Holman Christian Standard Bible, Copyright © 1999, 2000, 2003, 2009, Holman Bible Publishers; NLT are from the Holy Bible, New Living Translation, Copyright © 1996, Tyndale House Publishers, Inc, Wheaton, IL 60189; KJV are from the King James Version. All rights reserved. Used by permission.

ISBN-13: 978-0-9825719-4-1
ISBN-10: 0-9825719-4-1

First printing- October 2010

For Alvin Luther Autrey

November 21, 1937 - February 24, 2008

insquequo resurrection

"The generous soul will be made rich, and he who waters
will also be watered himself."
Proverbs 11:25 (NKJV)

"But seek first the kingdom of God and His righteousness,
and all these things shall be added to you."
Matthew 6:33 (NKJV)

"Give, and it shall be given to you. Good measure, pressed
down, shaken together, running over, will be put into your
lap. For with the measure you use it will be measured back
to you."
Luke 6:38 (ESV)

table of contents

author's note

Throughout this book are sprinkled song lyrics and movie quotes. These should not be understood as an endorsement of any specific song, artist, movie or actor. The purpose is to show, for good or ill, that money maintains a prominent place in our artistic culture. It is not something about which only preachers speak.

For purposes of reference, footnotes are numbered consecutively throughout and listed as endnotes. Numbers do not begin over with each chapter, which should make it simpler to locate any reference. Consecutive references to the same work are noted "Ibid." Non-consecutive references to the same work are listed with author's last name, title of work and page.

Events from my past have been recorded almost completely from memory. Any error is mine alone and wholly unintentional.

foreword

My granddaughter, Anna Grace, stood erect and proudly responded to her parents urging to recite her latest accomplishment of Scripture memory. She was four years old at the time and launched into a verbatim quoting of the Lord's Prayer. An occasional mispronunciation revealed the rote exercise may have lacked a clear understanding of its meaning. The wording, however, was perfect until she got to the closing. With her strongest childlike oratory she proclaimed, "For **mine** is the Kingdom and the power and the glory for **never** and **never**. Amen!"

She got the wording wrong, but the theology was exactly right. The kingdom of God is never about us. Most Christians would recognize that, but seldom is the concept reflected in our normal attitudes, behavior, and lifestyle. In spite of being undeserving recipients of God's grace and born into the Kingdom through faith in a Savior who came and purchased eternal redemption for us and a lost world, we tend to live for ourselves.

The psalmist puts it in perspective in reviewing the typical prayer of that ancient Hebrew age—one that continues to be prayed today, though perhaps in a more contemporary expression. "God be gracious to us and bless us, and cause His face to shine upon us" (Ps. 67:1). We want and expect God's blessings; in fact, we become impatient, disappointed and even bitter when God doesn't provide for our needs, and we have to go through times of austerity. But the reason God may choose to bless us is put in proper missional perspective in the verse that follows—"That Thy way may be made known on the earth, Thy salvation among all nations."

We typically pray for God to bless us, our family, our business, and every endeavor. We pray for Him to bless our church and its programs. But why should God choose to bless us, unless we use His blessings to be a blessing to others? We need to see God's favor, especially in financial success and material benefits, for the purpose of advancing His kingdom, witnessing to His salvation, and enabling us to minister in compassion to those in need.

In other words, we should not expect God's favor and grace if we are not committed to a missional lifestyle—using our wealth and financial capacity for His glory and purpose. This concept is graphically portrayed in *The Generous Soul: An Introduction to Missional Giving*. In a direct but appropriate style, Marty Duren will challenge you to a new level of generosity, highlighting the common discrepancy between trying to live a missional lifestyle without it being reflected in generous giving.

Having recently retired after seventeen years as president of the Southern Baptist International Mission Board, I find myself reflecting on the amazing advance of the gospel around the world. In God's providence, He is calling out missionaries in record numbers and is stirring a passion among churches to become aligned with His global activity to reach the nations. However, the decline in giving to missions has forced a tragic restriction in missionary appointments. Every survey reveals the number of tithers is diminishing, donations to charity are down, and even churches are consuming more of their budget resources on ingrown programs and elaborate facilities.

We have cleverly developed ways of justifying our lack of stewardship while presuming to live as obedient Christians, failing to realize that giving is probably the most authentic expression of our genuine devotion to Christ and His kingdom. We do not want to admit that the materialistic priorities to which most modern-day Christians have succumbed is nothing less than idolatry. The unprofitable servant who hid his talent and failed to use it in a way that would multiply its value was identified as "wicked." We think of wicked as being that which is evil and immoral, but is not this a proper characterization of the misuse of our wealth for self-indulgence rather than for God's mission and ministry?

It has been gratifying over the years to occasionally meet those who were missional givers. The power of their generosity was infectious. The joy of their life was unparalleled by those who had invested in every worldly amenity, though they chose personal austerity in order to give to others in need. They reflected the inextricable link between giving and living through a sensitivity to reach out to those who were hurting and in need. Their generosity invariably entailed personal sacrifice.

I was deeply moved visiting with a successful, young executive who had become a significant missions supporter. Tears streamed down his cheek as I shared testimonies of how God was moving in places of response around the world. He and his wife had prayed about becoming missionaries but never felt the convicting affirmation of God's call. He had been blessed incredibly in his investments and entrepreneurial skills, owning several businesses. His explanation for generous giving to missions was something I had never before encountered. He and his wife determined a basic budget of what they needed to live on and what they needed to put aside for their children's education. He pointed out that they determined any profit and income beyond that amount would be given to missions!

On another occasion I had been invited to make a presentation to a small foundation that was set up to support missions and evangelistic causes. The foundation leadership was quite impressed with the global scope of our work, but not being Southern Baptists, they were unfamiliar with our system of denomination support.

As I explained the SBC's Cooperative Program and an annual mission offering that provided our $300 million budget, it was an awkward context for appealing for a donation from their foundation. I said something to the effect of, "We are grateful for any resources you may want to channel to us, but we believe as long as we are obedient to God's mission and stay focused on the vision He has given, God will provide the resources we need."

The director of the foundation responded to remind me that we had not initiated this meeting, but that they had invited us to share about our work. He explained, "We are somewhat like a financial investment agency, but we are not looking for financial earnings; we are looking to invest in what will bring the greatest return in advancing the kingdom of God!"

That is the attitude that should motivate missional giving—recognizing that the financial resources at one's disposal are to be used for God's glory. It will open one's eyes to see beyond their own needs and desires, to see people in need and a lost world that needs to know Jesus.

The message of this book and the challenge of missional giving is clearly expressed in 1 John 3:17—"But whoever has the world's goods, and beholds his brother in need and closes his heart against him, how does the love of God abide in him?"

Jerry Rankin, President Emeritus
International Mission Board, SBC

introduction

Why this book?

One website states that 291,920 titles are published in the United States annually—more than 5,600 a week.[1] With so much to assimilate and so many from which to choose, why this book? Simply put, it needs to be written, and not because I am the one writing it. If this particular subject has been covered in this particular way, I've somehow missed it.

A recent visit to my local Christian bookstore's theology section revealed no books directly related to this subject. Some of the general theology books had no references to money, finances or stewardship, either in the table of contents or the index. The area of the store labeled *Finances* had plenty of books related to budgeting, debt elimination or investing as a Christian, but no books on the relationship between missional living and finances.

This should not be so.

Over the last decade or so, a thriving conversation has erupted around the concept of *missional*. It is a very important idea relating to how followers of Christ are to live in the world. Reams of pages have been written—not to estimate the number of 1s and 0s flung into cyberspace—exploring how Christians should relate to culture, what it means to be the church in a community, noting the difference between mission and missions, the nature of the gospel, ecclesiology, missiology, and on and on. It seems that almost every worthwhile connection has been made; many being profitably argued and others batted around *ad infinitum*.

One area that seems to have been explored to a lesser degree is how missional living relates to the financial responsibility of Christ's followers. Usually called stewardship, this sometimes overlooked and often loathed "money talk" is the bane of Christians in the West who spend an inordinate amount of time trying to justify purchases of excess clothing, housing, transportation, gaming, media, food, and other trinkets or toys. Yet, when Jesus wanted to draw a clear distinction between those who vie with God for our allegiance, one to whom we might submit the leading of our lives, He did not picture God opposed to ambitions, positions, or expressions, but possessions. He warned, "No one can serve two masters; for either he will hate the one and love the other, or he will be devoted to one and despise the other. You cannot serve God and wealth" (Matt. 6:24, NASB). Driscoll and Breshears rightfully note, "Money and wealth and possessions are among the greatest idols of our culture, and there is simply no way to be a disciple of Jesus apart from learning to worship God with stewardship."[2] In *Understanding Christian Theology*, Swindoll and Zuck assert that the development of stewardship in the believer is an evidence of sanctification (growing in Christ's likeness).[3]

The context of twenty-first century American life places us into a time when money is spent in astonishing ways. An August 2007 article on businessweek.com, relates:

If there's still any doubt whether the pampering of pets is getting out of hand, the debate should be settled once and for all by Neuticles, a patented testicular implant that sells for up to $919 a pair. The idea, says inventor Gregg A. Miller, is to 'let people restore their pets to anatomical preciseness' after neutering, thereby allowing them to retain their natural look and self-esteem. 'People thought I was crazy when I started 13 years ago,' says the Oak Grove (Mo.) entrepreneur. But he has since sold more than 240,000 pairs (a few of which went on prairie dogs, water buffalo, and monkeys). 'Neutering is creepy. But with Neuticles, it's like nothing has changed.' Nothing, except there's a fake body part where a real one used to be.[4]

Yes. You read that right. Nearly one thousand dollars to give animals fake parts to help their self-esteem. There is humor in this book, but that part is not a joke. Authors Diane Brady and Christopher Palmeri also report that Americans, as of 2006, spend forty-one billion dollars annually on buying, feeding and caring for pets, more than the GDP of over one hundred countries in the world.[5]

It does not seem we have come very far since Jim and Tammy Faye Bakker were mocked for air conditioning their dog's house, unless "in the wrong direction" is taken into account. More than a quarter-million sets of Neuticles proves that little is too extravagant for our pooches and kitties anymore. If only one year's worth of pet expenses were used, say, to install deep water wells in Africa, at thirty thousand dollars each,[6] around 1.4 billion wells could be built across that continent—more than one well for every man, woman and child. If only the $229 million spent on faux-testicles[7] had been used on African well projects, more than seven thousand deep water wells could have been dug. I just cannot imagine a scale where those disparities will ever balance.

Missional giving makes a financial priority of those things that are priorities in the kingdom of God: evangelism, justice, helping the poor, showing mercy, meeting needs, providing a cup of cold water in Jesus' name. Or some cash. Or cash from selling a car. Or a jet ski. Missional giving recognizes that all possessions entrusted to God's children are entrusted for the singular purpose of fulfilling God's plan. Missional giving approaches finances with the presupposition that Paul was telling the truth when he wrote, "My God shall supply all of your needs according to His riches in glory by Christ Jesus" (Phil. 4:19; NKJV). Missional giving does not recognize a dichotomy between God's money and my money. Instead, it forces the realization that all money and possessions belong to God and His children are channels through which Kingdom work is financed.

The proper understanding of finances means that the priorities of God's people related to money and possessions should be the same priorities that God has for the Kingdom. The use of money is not a separate reality from the gospel. On the contrary, our use of money and possessions is a direct reflection of our understanding of and love for the gospel and the Savior it reveals. If the gospel ("the Good News") is the story of God's redemptive activity through Jesus Christ of all things lost in the Fall, then everything under our management is usable for the embodiment and expansion of the gospel. If we keep money and possessions under a separate section of our lives it is tantamount to lording over that area ourselves rather than yielding lordship to Christ. To maintain this control of our finances is like divorcing ourselves from God. We cannot, no matter how much we try, serve both God and mammon.

As managers of God's possessions, our responsibility is to handle "our" stuff just as God would if He were on earth; this is the substance of Jesus' parables. With this in mind, I would offer this definition: *Missional giving is the financial strategy of the missionary manager, purposefully utilizing all the money and possessions God has entrusted to him or her according to His priorities and viewing all financial activity as integral with God's kingdom.*

Exploring these concepts is why this book exists.

part one

the theology of missional giving

or

what does my stuff have to do with God?

"Yours, O Lord, is the greatness, the power and the glory, the victory
and the majesty; for all that is in heaven and in earth is Yours; Yours is
the kingdom, O Lord, and You are exalted as head over all. Both
riches and honor come from You, and You reign over all. In Your
hand is power and might; in Your hand it is to make great and to give
strength to all."

I Chronicles 29:11, 12 (NKJV)

"God created the universe not as an object of academic scrutiny but as
an arena in which he can display something of his nature and
intentions."

Eugene Merrill
Everlasting Dominion[8]

chapter one

creation has its privileges

"For all the animals of the forest are mine, and I own the cattle on a
thousand hills. Every bird of the mountains and all the animals of the
field belong to me. If I were hungry, I would not mention it to you, for
all the world is mine and everything in it."

Psalm 50:10-12 (NLT)

"The earth is the Lord's, and everything in it. The world and all its
people belong to him."

Psalm 24:1 (NLT)

"MINE!!"

"NO, MINE!!!"

"Give. It. BACK!"

"NO!"

"I'm telling Mom!"

Who can forget those days, either from personal or parental experience? The desire to have and control displays itself at an early age. From the living room at home, to the church nursery, to the middle of the toy store, there is no place greed will not rear its green head. Some people eventually mature to an understanding about sharing and giving, while others grow old grasping and clutching. It is a battle each and every day of our lives to become givers rather than takers, rivers rather than reservoirs.

This tendency to grab and hold comes from our inherent feeling of ownership. Kids fight over dolls and action figures that barely have any temporal significance and none for eternity, while adults strive for bigger and better cars, houses, and toys of a different kind, which rarely have even the temporal significance we have attached to them. The late pastor-theologian A.W. Tozer addressed this condition:

There is within the human heart a tough, fibrous root of fallen life whose nature is to possess, always to possess. It covets things with a deep and fierce passion. The pronouns *my* and *mine* look innocent enough in print, but their constant and universal use is significant. They express the real nature of the old Adamic man better than a thousand volumes of theology could do. They are verbal symptoms of our deep disease.[9]

The more, more, more mindset was evidenced by the 1980's bumper sticker, "He who dies with the most toys wins," which was later edited to end with the single word "nothing" reflecting a more realistic view of time and eternity. Even so, the updating was a mere echo of Jesus Christ's warning in Luke, "Take care, and be on your guard against all covetousness, for one's life does not consist in the abundance of his possessions" (12:15, ESV).

As this chapter is being written (August 2010), Americans are being reminded in a rude way of the things we think we own but do not. Actual home repossessions have risen dramatically over the last three years of this economic downturn. In 2008, more than eight hundred thousand homes across the U.S. were repossessed. In 2009, the number was more than nine hundred thousand, and 2010 is projected to exceed one million.[10] These are not foreclosure filings, but actual repossessions. In neighborhoods all across the country, "home owners" are face to face with the fact that we do not own our homes until the last payment is made; until then the mortgage holder owns it. (Or, at least, some combination of speculators, banks and investment houses trading in mortgage-backed securities bundled with pork belly futures, shampoo bottles and coconut milk.)

You want to own it?

There are several ways to become an owner: create something, buy something, receive a gift, or inherit something are a few of them. If I walk into my basement, use my tools and my lumber to make a bench, it is mine until I give it away or sell it. It is mine because I created it. (And with my carpentry skills it is likely to remain mine for all time.) If you go to your local mall and give money in exchange for a book, item of home decor, or clothing, it becomes yours by right of purchase. It no longer belongs to the store; it belongs to you until you give it away or sell it. If a relative dies and leaves a pristine 1965 Mustang to your brother-in-law and a less-than-pristine 1977 Pacer to you, the Pacer is yours (until you convince your brother-in-law of the benefits to him of a straight-up trade).

The Bible records in its opening verse, "In the beginning God created the heavens and the earth" (Gen. 1:1, NASB). By virtue of creation, God owns everything in the universe. He created it; it belongs to Him. The farthest star and the nearest atom are His alike. The widest mountain and thinnest blades of grass bear the indelible *imprateur* of His ownership. Given the vastness of our universe, it should come as no surprise that the record of God's creation activity is not limited to the initial book of the Bible. Ken Hemphill writes, "[The word *created*] so permeates the Bible that it is found dotted throughout the Scripture—twenty times alone in chapters 40-66 of Isaiah. If you read that section, you will discover that the prophet was intent on distinguishing between Israel's God as the true Lord of history—its Creator—in contrast to the Babylonian practices of idolatry and astrology."[11]

The reasons for such an emphasis should not be lost on us today. Though the existence of an all powerful God was questioned even in ancient days,[12] naturalism since Darwin has set its deity-denying sights on the anything that hints of God's special creation of the universe. If special creation by the biblical God is removed, then there is no God to make a claim to ownership anyway, so everyone may as well live as they wish.[13]

Question and question time

The Old Testament book of Job records a rather blunt sermon God once preached to His servant, the man named Job. Throughout the course of a brutal Q&A in chapter 38 of that book—which proved to be substantially more Q than A—God repeatedly staked His ownership claim on creation by reminding Job who had made it in the first place. "Where were you when I laid the foundation of the earth? Who set its measurements? Since you know, or who stretched the line on it? On what were its bases sunk? Or who laid its cornerstone?" (vs. 4-6); "And I placed boundaries on [the sea] and set a bolt and doors, and I said, 'Thus far you shall come, but no farther; and here shall your proud waves stop'?" (vs. 10, 11). Nor did God stop with His earthly creativity. In the second half of the chapter, He went NASA on His quieted questioner: "Can you bind the chains of the Pleiades, or loose the cords of Orion? Can you lead forth a constellation in its season, and guide the Bear with her sons? Do you know the ordinances of the heavens, or fix their rule over the earth?" (vs. 31-33. All verses NASB). God claims ownership of everything by way of creation and He is not outside the bounds in doing so.

Through the next several chapters of Job, God claimed authority over animals, weather patterns, and humanity. And why should He not? He created all that is seen and unseen; the visible world of our habitation and the invisible world of His. From sub-atomic particles and strings (if indeed they exist) to the massive star R126a1, which is suspected to be 265 times larger than our sun.[14] It all came from the creative power of His Word.

In the Psalms, God reminds us of the reality of His ownership: The cattle on a thousand hills belong to Him.[15] The gold and the silver belong to Him.[16] In other words, the substance for our subsistence belongs to God not to us. The sources of our food belong to Him and the sources for our finances belong to Him. We created none of it, He has not placed any of it up for sale, therefore, we own none of it; we merely use it by His grace. The church father, Irenaeus, recognized that all things come from God, saying, "God is the commencement of all. He comes from no one, and all things come from Him...Among all things is included what we call the world, and in the world man."[17] And, despite the sorry condition of the world's economy at present, there are no liens on God's property.

But what about me?

At this point someone might argue, "But God did not build that house I just flipped. Neither did He work hard to close that business deal at the end of last week. Can He really claim ownership of all the things that have happened since the end of creation?" He can and He does, rightfully so. We cannot claim to be productive in business or successful in moneymaking apart from God.

> Big money goes
> around the world
>
> Big money
> underground
>
> Big money got a
> mighty voice
>
> Big money make
> no sound
>
> Big money pull a
> million strings
>
> Big money hold
> the prize
>
> Big money weave
> a mighty web
>
> Big money draws
> the flies
>
> "Big Money"
> Rush

In the Old and New Testaments, God makes it plain that those abilities are graciously given from Him. Moses warned the children of Israel by way of this reminder,

"In the wilderness He fed you with manna which your fathers did not know, that He might humble you and that He might test you, to do good for you in the end. Otherwise, you may say in your heart, 'My power and the strength of my hand made me this wealth.' But you shall remember the Lord your God, for it is He who is giving you power to make wealth, that He may confirm His covenant which He swore to your fathers, as it is this day."[18]

Blaise Pascal addressed this thorough dependence we have on God: "All things on earth show man's wretchedness and God's mercy, man's helplessness without God and man's power with God."[19]

The apostle James recognized the tendency within us to regard our business dealings as our own. His pastoral admonition to the scattered early believers reads,

"Come now, you who say, 'Today or tomorrow we will go to such and such a city, spend a year there, buy and sell, and make a profit'; whereas you do not know what will happen tomorrow. For what is your life? It is even a vapor that appears for a little time and then vanishes away. Instead, you ought to say, 'If the Lord wills, we shall live and do this or that.' But now you boast in your arrogance. All such boasting is evil" (James 4:13-16; NKJV).

James does not merely suggest that we should give priority to God in our business dealings, but that to not do so is evil arrogance. Why? Because God is owner, therefore any productivity in business, agriculture or other moneymaking comes from His hand alone.

Though his name, for many, is not instantly recognizable today, the late R.G. LeTourneau credited God for everything about his very

successful business. Called the "Mover of Mountains and Men,"
LeTourneau was the holder of 299 inventions related to bulldozers,
earthmovers, oil drilling, logging equipment and others. During World
War II, his companies produced 70 percent of all the U.S. Army's
earth-moving machinery. With a heart beating for the Kingdom, he
often spoke of God as the Chairman of his Board.[20] Despite his
wealth, LeTourneau recognized who owned it all.

Ownership in the parables

Consider how the parables of Jesus portray God's relationship to
humanity as it concerns ownership: God is always the owner of the
land or vineyard, while we are pictured as tenants, workers, or
managers. In the parable of the unforgiving servant,[21] God is the king
who has full authority over the possessions of a debtor servant. In the
parable of the unjust steward,[22] God is the rich man who demands an
accounting from His servant. In the parable of the two sons,[23] He is
the father who owns the vineyard and tells both of his sons to work in
it. In the parable of the faithful servant,[24] God is the man who went to
a far country, leaving his servants with authority over his house. In the
parable of the talents[25] (one of the most well known), the owner
delegates financial responsibilities to some of his servants, with varying
results.

Just the start

While this is not a comprehensive review of the Bible's teaching on
this subject, it is representative of the whole. In other words, "There's
more where that came from." One would be hard pressed to read the
Bible and conclude that we own anything. God owns it all; we own
nothing at all. When Jesus spoke of the poor in spirit, He revealed the

meaning of true possession. He said, "Blessed are the poor in spirit, for theirs is the kingdom of heaven."[26] A.W. Tozer explains, "[The] blessed poor are no longer slaves to the tyranny of things. They have broken the yoke of the oppressor.... Though free from all sense of possessing, they yet possess all things. 'Theirs is the kingdom of heaven.'"[27]

In addition to God's ownership by virtue of creation, He has an ownership claim by virtue of His sustaining power. It is to this truth that we now turn.

meditations

Using the following space, reflect on what Scripture impacted you the most in this chapter. What response does God require of you?

chapter two

providence is not just a city in Rhode Island

"O LORD, how manifold are Your works! In wisdom You have made
them all. The earth is full of your possessions."
Psalm 104:24 (NKJV)

"Who has given to Me that I should repay him? Whatever is under the
whole heaven is Mine."
Job 41:11 (ESV)

People see God every day; they just don't recognize Him.
Pearl Bailey

"Dad, I've been in an accident."

The first time you hear those words, the immediate mental response runs to every form of injury ever witnessed on *COPS* or one of those Japanese full body cast game shows. Then you think, "Wait, he's on the phone. This isn't a police officer calling. He must be OK." The second time you hear those words you think, "There go my insurance premiums."

In June 2010, my son had an accident that totaled his car. We were thankful that he walked away unscathed, literally without even a seatbelt burn. No other car was severely damaged, but his radiator and front grill was pushed back into the engine. The repair would have been far more than the car was ever going to be worth so we scrapped it and walked away with two hundred dollars. When we cancelled the insurance on it we got a few dollars in refund money.

I kept it all. It was not much and it only went to other expenses, but I kept it. It was "his car," but he never saw a dime of that money.

Many parents have the experience of "giving" a child a car while retaining ownership. The name of one or both parents is on the title, the insurance and the tag. The parents pay the payments, the maintenance, the repairs, and some if not all of the gasoline. At the same time, the parents say, "That is Sarah's car," or "Ben, will you please wash your truck?" What it really means is that Sarah and Ben have many of the *privileges* of ownership while we retain almost all the *responsibilities* of ownership.

What parent has not said in a moment of frustration or discipline, "Don't forget who owns that car! It is my name on the title. I pay the insurance and maintain that car. I can take it away if you don't do what I say." It is a common sentiment, one that some young drivers need to hear regularly.

And it's true. I claim ownership of the car because I maintain it.

God as sustainer

God's ownership of this world is claimed not only because He created the universe, but also because He maintains it. He does not fight with man, angels, demons, or Satan over ownership. Paul reminds us that Jesus Christ, the second Person of the Godhead, maintains this physical world. "By Him everything was created, in heaven and on earth, the visible and the invisible, whether thrones or dominions or rulers or authorities—all things have been created through Him and for Him, He is before all things, and by Him all things hold together" (Col. 1:16, 17; HCSB). The writer of Hebrews said that God made the universe through Jesus and that Jesus "sustains the universe by the mighty power of his command" (Heb. 1:3; NLT). The same word of God that created the universe sustains the universe. If God were to remove His sustaining power, the universe would either explode into debris or implode into nothingness. Either way, it would not be a very pretty sight.

God's sustaining power is seen, for instance, in the use of "Almighty" and "mighty" with His name. Martin Luther writes, "The word 'mighty' does not denote a quiescent power, as one says of a temporal king that he is mighty, even though he be sitting and doing nothing. But it denotes *an energetic power, a continuous activity*, that works and operates without ceasing...as Christ says in John 5, 'My Father is working until now, and I am working.'"[28] God is not like a self-indulgent king sprawled across a throne being cooled by servants waving palm fronds all day long. Nor is He like Luther's image, looking out a window bored out of His skull. He is active, powerful and mighty.

Thomas Oden recounts the scope of God's sustaining power (what he and others call *providence*) saying, "No creature is so great as to be beyond the need of God's care (Ps. 103)...No creature is so small as to be overlooked by God's care: ravens (Ps. 147:9), sparrows (Matt. 10:29), lilies and grass (Matt. 6:28, 30), and the hairs of our heads (Matt. 10:30). God's providential sustenance embraces the physical world (Job 37:5), animal creation (Ps. 104:21), the affairs of nations (Isa. 40:ff), [and] justice in societies (Job 12:16-25; Amos 5)...Nothing is beyond God's providence."[29] Since God's providence is responsible for sustaining every single thing in creation, even the grass in my front yard belongs to Him; or, in the case of desert dwellers, the cacti growing there.

God's sustaining power has also been called *preservation* by other writers and theologians through the years. A.H. Strong, for instance, writes,

> Forget your lust
> for rich man's
> gold
>
> All that you need
> is in your soul
>
> And you can do
> this if you try
>
> All I want for you
> my son
> is to be satisfied
>
> "Simple Kind of
> Man"
> Lynyrd Skynyrd

"Preservation is that continuous agency of God by which he maintains in existence the things he has created, together with the properties and powers with which he has endowed them...Preservation is not a mere negation of action, or a refraining to destroy, on the part of God. It is a positive agency by which, at every moment, he sustains the persons and the forces of the universe."[30]

In other words, God's sustaining power is not simply that God does not do something, like destroy the world with a large piece of space flotsam, but that He positively promotes and provides for His creation.

I remember as a child hearing people say things like, "Yes, I'll be at the meeting if I am not Providentially hindered." That to which the person referred was God's sustaining power over His creation, His providence. If, in the working of God in the world the person was allowed to be at the meeting, he or she would be there. "I do not have any other plans," they could have said, "but God might. My attendance depends on my plans and His."

> Money talks
>
> But it can't sing and dance
>
> And it don't walk.
>
> "Forever in Blue Jeans"
> Neil Diamond

It is worth noting that God's sustaining is not merely a tyrant's claim on something He owns. Instead, He interacts with His creation and, specifically, humanity. Eugene Merrill reminds us, "The core, unifying theme of Old Testament theology is the reigning of God...The Bible presents him as independently sovereign, answerable to no one and in need of nothing or no one outside himself. But *it also presents him as in vital contact with all he has made, especially with mankind, that part of the creation made uniquely as his own image.*"[31] We need look no further than the incarnation of God in Jesus Christ to see this interaction personalized and intensified in the New Testament. No more "vital contact" could be desired than that God would become a man and live among humanity for thirty-three years. It is this caring (and redemptive) interaction with humanity that keeps the sustaining power of God (His providence or preservation) from degenerating into the faceless, impersonal mythology of the fates. *Que sera, sera*[32] is not what will be; what God sustains and oversees will be.[33]

Are we not talking about miracles?

Many Christians and unbelievers alike are familiar with the miracles recorded in the Bible. A miracle is generally thought of as a time when God suspends physical laws to meet a need (as in providing manna) or to demonstrate His power (Elijah calling fire from heaven).[34] The crossing of the Red Sea,[35] making the sun stand still,[36] the slaughter of Sennacherib's army,[37] and the feeding of the five thousand[38] are where our minds tend to turn when we think of miracles. If a miracle is God's special intervention, providence may be thought of as God's non-miraculous guidance. It would be this sustaining, providence, and preservation that the author of the proverb referenced when writing, "The lot is cast into the lap, but its every decision is from the LORD" (Prov. 16:33; NKJV).

God is able to provide this kind of consistent and ongoing providence because—and only because—He is the owner of all that is. He need not run to another for permission since His ability is within His infinite being. The psalmist could thus observe, "I was young and now I am old, yet I have never seen the righteous forsaken or their children begging bread" [Ps. 37:25; NIV].

The Fatherly God

There is in this a clear parallel to good parenting. Good parents sustain their children by purchasing food, clothes, school supplies, and other needs. Children brought into this world bring parental responsibilities. "I helped create this little life so I have a responsibility to sustain this little life." The same holds true, of course, for adopted children. Jesus used the metaphor of God's fatherhood in the context of prayer and provision. In Matthew, He taught, "You parents—if your children ask for a loaf of bread, do you give them a stone instead? Of course not! If you sinful people know how to give good gifts to your children, how much more will your heavenly Father give good gifts to those who ask him" (Matt. 7: 9-11; NLT). If we are able to sustain our children, how much more is God able to do so? If you are God's child through faith in Jesus Christ, then you are not excluded from the faithful fatherhood of God.

So, the Scripture teaches that God is owner by virtue of creation, and His ownership is repeatedly confirmed by His providence. The proper response to God for His ownership of all things is a right relationship to those things, but a battle ensues over those allegiances.

meditations

Using the following space, reflect on what Scripture impacted you the most in this chapter. What response does God require of you?

chapter three

the ghost of mammon present

"If you was to make a real strike, you couldn't be dragged away. Not
even the threat of miserable death would keep you from trying to add
ten thousand more. Ten you'd want to get twenty-five, twenty-five
you'd want to get fifty, fifty a hundred. Like roulette. One more turn,
you know. Always one more."

Howard (Walter Huston)

The Treasure of the Sierra Madre

"There's a whole ocean of oil under our feet!
No one can get at it except for me!"

Daniel Plainview (Daniel Day-Lewis)

There Will Be Blood

"Little children, keep yourselves from idols."

I John 5:21 (NKJV)

Scrooge had had a looooong night. What he surmised would be another cold winter evening alone by the fire was interrupted by the chained, head-wrapped ghost of his former business partner, Jacob Marley. Lest Scrooge feel relieved too quickly in hoping for the departure of Marley's ghost, the specter promised that Scrooge would have an entire night of interruptions. Three more spirits would visit Scrooge, replaying his past, reiterating his present, and revealing his future.

With increasing futility, the tight-walleted financier made excuses for his greed and covetousness. Finally, with morning about to dawn, Scrooge was led by the Ghost of Christmas Yet to Come to a place most repugnant. Dickens describes the scene: "[Scrooge] recognised its situation, and its bad repute. The ways were foul and narrow; the shops and houses wretched; the people half-naked, drunken, slip-shod, ugly. Alleys and archways, like so many cesspools, disgorged their offences of smell, and dirt, and life, upon the straggling streets; and the whole quarter reeked with crime, with filth and misery."[39]

Disgustedly Scrooge watched as the thieves, beggars and broken bartered the goods they secured during the day's scrounging. To his horror he saw some of the goods were from his own home, taken after his death. Buttons, a watch and bed-curtains contributed to the chattle of this bizarre bazaar as the traders joked ruthlessly at the expense of Scrooge's reputation. Or perhaps because of it. He finally demanded of the Spirit to see tenderness, to see depth of feeling rather than the callous display of worldliness he had been forced to witness. The best the phantom could do, though, was to take Scrooge to a couple rejoicing because the miser no longer held their debt. They reckon "it would be bad fortune indeed to find so merciless a creditor in his successor. We may sleep tonight with light hearts!"[40]

Sneak attack

Do you grovel to your master?

Do you beg like a dog?

First things first, repeat to yourself

Ahhh money! Money is not our god!

"Money is Not Our God"
Killing Joke

In the rare times when we do evaluate ourselves, we too easily assign covetousness to those like Scrooge, the notorious miser Hetty Green,[41] or others we feel are doing a better than exceptional job of misdirecting their treasures. Carefully we categorize our needs as genuine, our wants as necessities and draw ambiguously blurred lines between the excesses of covetousness and what we must have in order to live; that is, our genuine needs. Without warning our wants morph into perceived needs with a 1080p, flatscreen TV suddenly sharing equal billing with groceries for the family. It is with good reason that Tim Keller lists money as one of our counterfeit gods. Keller writes, "Innumerable writers and thinkers have been pointing out 'the culture of greed' that has been eating away at our souls and has brought about economic collapse. Yet no one thinks that change is around the corner. Why? It's because greed and avarice are especially hard to see in ourselves."[42] "Satan well knows that, generally speaking, to try to ensnare real Christians through things that are positively sinful is vain and futile," wrote the Chinese evangelist Watchman Nee.[43] Craig Groeschel agrees, "Trusting in money generally sneaks up on us."[44]

Perhaps because of the insidious nature of covetousness God chose to include it in the Ten Commandments; we need to be on constant guard. Groeschel also calls money our "functional savior."[45] A functional savior is the one we turn to in times of need and our material possessions easily fill in the "need gap." We need an eternal savior when we stand before the judgment so we claim Christ, but, in our daily lives we too often turn to that which is more tangible: possessions.

It is not, however, mere instructions about how to balance a budget or make investments that are foundational in our relationship to possessions. If possessions (wealth, mammon) can actually be a master in our lives, then we are dealing with emotional and spiritual submission toward a false god, not simply bad investment advice or choices between which car to buy. Like any false god, possessions cannot hear, speak, give life direction, or help us. They are deaf, dumb and blind, as are those who are submitted to them.[46] While more fashionable than worshiping Baal or Amimitl, the worship of mammon is the same foolish dead end.

Idolatry? In the twenty-first century?

Paul warned the Colossians that covetousness was the same as idolatry,[47] but this is rarely how Christians think about it today. Like Pavlov's pooches we drool on command over every electronics sale paper, new car advertisement, or 30 percent off coupon at the local clothing store, but we rarely think of it as idolatry. This is a heinous error since covetousness—greed, unbridled desire—*is* the same as idol worship. Keyes notes, "An idol is something within creation that is inflated to function as a substitute for God." These are the very idols about which Jeremiah warned, "For the customs of the peoples are worthless; they cut a tree out of the forest, and a craftsman shapes it with his chisel. They adorn it with silver and gold; they fasten it with hammer and nails so it will not totter. Like a scarecrow in a melon patch, their idols cannot speak; they must be carried because they cannot walk. Do not fear them; they can do no harm nor can they do any good" (Jer. 10:3-5; NIV).

Wait...idolatry? For real? Yes, as John R.W. Stott concludes, "Anybody who divides his allegiance between God and mammon has already given it to mammon, since God can be served only with an entire and exclusive devotion...To try to share him with other loyalties is to have opted for idolatry."[48] The modern equivalent to the god *mammon* about which Jesus warned is *materialism*. The Encarta World English Dictionary defines it as "devotion to material wealth and possessions at the expense of spiritual or intellectual values."[49] Note carefully the use of the word *devotion*; it is an emotional connection made with things. An atheist might define materialism as "the idea that everything is either made only of matter or is ultimately dependent upon matter for its existence and nature."[50] It can be thought of as the religion of those who reject belief in God; it is closely related to naturalism, "a system of thought that rejects all spiritual and supernatural explanations of the world and holds that science is the sole basis of what can be known."[51] It should be easy to see why Jesus made such a clear distinction: the worship of *things* equals the abandonment of the true God for idols.

There goes the neighborhood

Imagine that you arrive home one night just after dark to a roaring fire in the backyard of your next-door neighbor, who himself is stripped naked with skin glistening in mud and blood smeared from head to toe. Moments later his similarly adorned wife emerges from their home with a sharpened chef's knife and their two-month-old child. With the blood draining from your own head, you watch as their child is murdered, then offered in the flames to the pagan god Molech. The virtual certainty that we will never witness this kind of scenario helps us form a barrier as to the true nature of idolatry, even as the love of money and possessions form an idolatry that differs in style but not in substance.

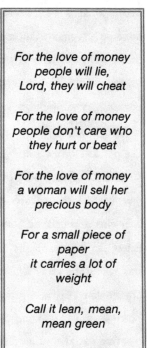

*For the love of money
people will lie,
Lord, they will cheat*

*For the love of money
people don't care who
they hurt or beat*

*For the love of money
a woman will sell her
precious body*

*For a small piece of
paper
it carries a lot of
weight*

*Call it lean, mean,
mean green*

Almighty dollar

"For the Love of Money"
The O'Jays

When Paul warned those early believers of the idolatrous nature of covetousness, i.e., greed, he was not merely practicing the rhetorical flourishes of a former Pharisee trying not to lose his touch. He was speaking in a culture still fully aware of the nature of false gods, from images of rock and stone to the emperor of Rome. Every Christian anywhere in the Roman Empire was exposed to and familiar with idolatry. Though twenty-first century Americans are, by way of the calendar, far removed from the Roman Empire, our idolatry is just as real. We are kissing cousins even if we will not admit it. Harold O.J. Brown warns of our materialistic bent, proposing that we have become a "sensate culture," that is, a culture that "is interested only in those things, usually material in nature, that appeal to or affect the senses. It seeks the imposing, the impressive, the voluptuous; it encourages self-indulgence."[52] He continues, "No apology is made for encouraging people to squander their resources on self-indulgence. Let us 'eat, drink and be merry,' forgetting that 'tomorrow we die.' Sensate culture...[goes] beyond simple materialism in that materialism merely defines matter as the only reality; the sensate mentality becomes enthusiastic about it."[53] The Corinthians were told that the Epicurean philosophy of "Let us eat and drink, for tomorrow we die" was accurate only if there is no resurrection (1 Cor. 15:32). Theologian Wayne Grudem agrees: "The fact that creation is distinct from God yet always dependent on God, that God is far above creation yet always involved in it...[is] clearly distinct from *materialism*, which is the most common philosophy of unbelievers today, and which denies the existence of God altogether."[54] Where there is no God, everything becomes god.[55]

Too much junk in the trunk

If the way that Christians give money to Kingdom purposes is any indicator (and it is not just *any* indicator, it is a *primary* one), then we have long ago become "enthusiastic" about materialism (to use Brown's term) even though it is financial atheism. When we need God, we pray and beg His blessing, but our possessions leave us believing that we rarely need God. We budget, spend, and borrow as if there is no God nor ever has been. Our homes are as large and well-appointed as those of unbelievers, our cars as expensive and frequently traded, our clothes bear the same branded labels, our conventions in the same cities and hotels, our gizmos as intricate and pricey—there is virtually no difference between the rank atheist and the "follower of Christ" when possessions are the measure. An honest examination would reveal that we have traded God for things, laughing all the way to the bank. We are not simply observers in the worship of mammon, we stand with arms high and hearts abandoned![56]

A friend recently called relating an incident that happened during a meeting at his work. The owner, a professing Christian, told the agents in attendance, "Greed is good." If a believer, this businessman would find himself in some rather questionable company. Besides the obvious reference to Gordon Gekko (Michael Douglas) from the movie *Wall Street*, the renowned anti-theist, Christopher Hitchens said in a 2009 documentary, "Coveting your neighbor's goods [is] a perfectly healthy thing to do."[57] When believers find themselves joining atheists in calling sin "good" and "healthy," the problem cannot be overstated.

Once when a rich young man came to Jesus[58] asking the way of salvation, Jesus hit him right in the heart (not like wrestling or Bon Jovi; like the Holy Spirit): "Sell everything that you have, give it to the poor and follow me," He said. This was never the norm in the gospels nor in the balance of the New Testament; nowhere is poverty extolled as more virtuous than wealth.[59] In this man's life, however, it had to be the centerpiece of his repentance. His god was mammon; his possessions ruled his life. It was not that the young man was a philandering, sensually indulgent pig; on the contrary, he affirmed his personal, law-keeping morality. When Jesus asked about his adherence to the commandments, he replied, "Master, all these I have kept from my youth up." In their New York Times bestseller, *Freakonomics*, Leavitt and Dubner write, "Morality, it could be argued, represents the way that people would like the world to work—whereas economics represents how it actually *does* work."[60] Their thesis is a perfect description of the young man's struggle. He was looking for moral rightness, but his economics told the story; he could not get beyond his money and get to Jesus.

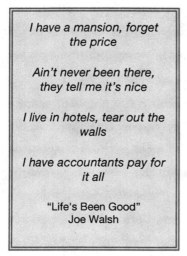

I have a mansion, forget the price

Ain't never been there, they tell me it's nice

I live in hotels, tear out the walls

I have accountants pay for it all

"Life's Been Good"
Joe Walsh

Jesus' treatment of the rich young man was no different than if a Baal worshiper had come seeking eternal life. Jesus might well have responded, "Turn your back on Baal, trash all your Baal idols, then follow me." It would have been an equivalent instruction; an idol is an idol is an idol.

The difference here is in the fact that the Baal idol needing to be trashed is sitting *on* the fireplace mantle, while the possession Jesus commanded the young man to sell *was* the fireplace mantle. And the fireplace...and the house...and the furniture...and the property. You get the idea. Jesus never presented following Him as an easy thing; it means the dethroning of every idol. Since we tend to more closely identify with the idols of the rich young man, we hope and pray it was a one-shot deal. Otherwise we might have to become homeless to follow Christ. Who would want to do that? Yet, Jesus was clear about the cost. When Peter reminded Jesus of all that His disciples had left to follow Him, Jesus only affirmed that there would be a reward, not that their abandonment of "everything" was unnecessary.[61]

(Now before you throw this book into the recycle bin expecting that a call is coming to sell everything that you have and give it to your church's building fund or the Red Cross, don't pass out; that is not where this is going. It is not where most people need to go. However, to get where we need to go, we have to deal with what is keeping us from getting there, and what is keeping us from getting there is pretty deeply ingrained. We will consider later whether the worship of mammon has actually been integrated into our worldview.)

> The best things in
> life are free
>
> But you can give
> them to the birds
> and bees
>
> I want money
>
> Your love gives
> me such a thrill
>
> But your love
> won't pay my bills
>
> I want money
>
> Give me your
> money
>
> Just give me
> money
>
> "Money"
> The Flying Lizards

Why it goes wrong and where

The war between materialism and the kingdom of God is all the more difficult because it is a war between the seen and the unseen. Money is tangible, possessions usable, bank and stock accounts reviewable, debit and credit cards holdable. All of these things can war against faith, which strives to see that which is invisible, lives in the hope of eternity, holds to a God who is transcendent, and emphasizes the existence of *the* reality of which what we see are mere shadows and smoke. It was this feature that moved C.S. Lewis to call this earthly home the "shadowlands." So what happens when we start treating the shadows like the substance? It should be obvious; we are left with nothing.

Visualeconomics.com recently featured a breakdown of how the average American consumer disposes of his or her annual income.

Well, it's a bittersweet symphony, this life

Try to make ends meet you're a slave to money then you die

"Bittersweet Symphony"
The Verve

Based on a U.S. Department of Labor survey, the breakdown reveals that Americans spend 5.4 percent of after-tax income on entertainment, the same amount that is spent going out to eat. Cash contributions (including the tithes and offerings of Christians) equal 3.7 percent ($1,821/yr), just less than the amount spent on alcohol, tobacco, personal care, and "miscellaneous."[62] The practical reality of giving 3.7 percent provides a stark contrast to a Kingdom expected to consume 100 percent of our lives and the King who requires it. (One organization, Giving USA, using the GDP as a baseline, says our giving was 2.2 percent in 2008, just less than the 2.3 percent in 2007.[63])

We will not see the spread of the gospel to those who have never heard when we are more financially committed to movie tickets.

All that preacher talks about...

For years, members of Western churches have complained, "All the preacher ever talks about is money." Sometimes these missiles of negativity are launched with good reason; the capital campaign that is not reaching the mark results in a weekly scathing to "dig deep" and "give more." It can get tiresome. Realistically, though, there can scarcely be a more needed reminder for us. Perhaps we do need more sermons on the right handling of possessions than on murder, adultery, and jihad. Are we to believe that there are more murderers in attendance on a typical Sunday morning than those who have misspent God's money? More adulterers than the covetous? A greater number of imminent suicide bombers than thieves? A larger portion of those laying up for themselves treasures in heaven than those laying up treasures in the garage, family room or walk-in closet? If our false god is mammon, then we need to be called out regularly for following that idol.

John Piper writes, "Money is the currency of human resources...So the

> *Money, get away.*
>
> *Get a good job with good pay and you're okay.*
>
> *Money, it's a gas.*
>
> *Grab that cash with both hands and make a stash.*
>
> *New car, caviar, four-star daydream,*
>
> *Think I'll buy me a football team.*
>
> "Money"
> Pink Floyd

heart that loves money is a heart that pins its hopes, and pursues its pleasure, and puts its trust in what human resources can offer. So the love of money is virtually the same as faith in money or belief (trust, confidence, assurance) that money will meet your needs and make you happy."[64] Even the folksy wisdom of Benjamin Franklin teaches us better than to believe that: "Money never made a man happy yet, nor will it. There is nothing in its nature to produce happiness. The more a man has, the more he wants. Instead of it filling a vacuum, it makes one. If it satisfies one want, it doubles and triples that want another way."[65] The "Preacher" wrote much the same thing in the Old Testament book of Ecclesiastes, "He who loves money will not be satisfied with money, nor he who loves wealth with his income; this also is vanity"(5:10; ESV).

Perhaps the reason Jesus pitted God against mammon in the Sermon on the Mount is because He knew this devastating, vacuous nature of materialism. To serve things is to commit both idolatry and adultery. It is idolatry because we submit ourselves to its lordship, but it is adultery because we are already married to another.[66] It is not too far a stretch to call it prostitution since, in both instances, the affections are bought with money. The Old Testament prophet Hosea's marriage to the unfaithful Gomer was the visual God used to picture of Israel's playing the harlot. How much more drastic would God's visual have to be today to picture the way American believers have betrayed the vows with our heavenly spouse? The Lutheran martyr Dietrich Bonhoeffer described it in these blunt terms, "Whoredom is the first sin against the Creator,"[67] while Tozer concluded, "The roots of our hearts have grown down into things, and we dare not pull up one rootlet lest we die. *Things have become necessary to us*, a development never originally intended. God's gifts now take the place of God, and the whole course of nature is upset by the monstrous substitution."[68]

The good news is that, like all things of God, there is a better way. The proper relationship between God, possessions, and ourselves centers us in the stream of God's mission and releases us from the burdens of ownership into the blessings of missionary management.

meditations

Using the following space, reflect on what Scripture impacted you the most in this chapter. What response does God require of you?

part two

the missiology of missional giving

or

does God have a plan for my stuff?

"For of Him and through Him and to Him are all things. To whom be
glory forever. Amen."
Romans 11:36 (NKJV)

"Whoever can be trusted with very little can also be trusted with
much, and whoever is dishonest with very little will also be dishonest
with much. So if you have not been trustworthy in handling worldly
wealth, who will trust you with true riches?"
Luke 16:10, 11 (NIV)

"All too often, I fear, we are bad givers. If I am only a receiver and not
also a giver, I am unworthy of the God who sent me. The divine
principle is not 'Save and you shall grow rich.' It is 'Give and it shall be
given unto you.'"
Watchman Nee
A Table in the Wilderness[69]

chapter four

missionary managers

"Money, pardon the expression, is like manure. It's not worth a thing
unless it's spread around, encouraging things to grow."

Dolly Levi (Barbra Streisand)
Hello Dolly!

"Do not value money for any more nor any less than its worth; it is a
good servant but a bad master."

Alexander Dumas

"'What then should we do?' the crowds were asking [John].
He replied to them, 'The one who has two shirts must share with
someone who has none, and the one who has food must do the
same.'"

Luke 3:10, 11 (HCSB)

It is difficult for a follower of Christ not to be moved by a missionary story. From the earliest moments of salvation, it seems stories are relayed about the faithful lives and sometimes deaths of those intrepid servants of God who left most—if not all—in pursuit of souls. David Brainerd, Adoniram Judson, Hudson Taylor, Amy Carmichael, Gladys Aylward, Stan Dale, Phil Masters, Lottie Moon, Bill Wallace, John Paton, Mary Slessor, and countless others have inspired believers for centuries. What believer, having heard the story of Jim Elliot, Nate Saint, Ed McCully, Roger Youderian, Pete Fleming, Elizabeth Elliot, Rachel Saint and, now, Steve Saint, has not marveled at the grace and wisdom of God among the Huaorani people and been challenged in his or her own spiritual journey.[70]

Meeting with missionaries on their field of service is always a humbling experience. Crowded around a kitchen table or crammed three-people-too-many into a small car, listening to the stories of call, training, and experiences are enough to warm any cold heart. Some of the richest "God moments" of my entire life have taken place in these kinds of situations. I think the lack of these times constitutes a hole in the spiritual development of many believers.

On the move

The gospel of Matthew contains what is generally referenced as "The Great Commission," those words of Jesus preparing His disciples for their mission, which soon would become a reality.[71] In Acts 1:8,

Jesus informed the disciples that they would be witnesses to Him (meaning His life, death, and resurrection), beginning where they lived and continuing across the entire world. Over time, this is exactly what happened. In fact, two millennia later, you and I came to faith in Christ as a result of their initial obedience.

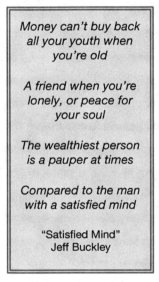

Money can't buy back all your youth when you're old

A friend when you're lonely, or peace for your soul

The wealthiest person is a pauper at times

Compared to the man with a satisfied mind

"Satisfied Mind"
Jeff Buckley

As long as those early followers were in predominantly Jewish areas, they were able to tell the story of Jesus among Jewish people using Jewish history and Jewish ideals, hopes and expectations, explaining that Jesus the Jewish rabbi was Jesus Christ the world's Messiah. As they moved out farther into the Roman Empire, where cultures began to be mixed or distinctly different, it was common to utilize some of those particular cultural forms to share the gospel. They did not change the message, but they did use word pictures and ideas familiar to their audience so the truth was communicated. These—Paul, Barnabas, Mark, Silas—are thought of as some of the first Christian missionaries.

Over time, the idea has taken hold that only those fitting this kind of criteria *are* missionaries. It will be helpful to determine whether this idea fully squares with Scripture.

On the move?

The scriptural record seems clear that all followers of Christ are missionaries no matter their country, culture, or context. God is a sending God and we are a sent people. Jesus said, "As the Father has sent me, so I am sending you."[72] Like John the Baptist we are sent "from God."[73] We may not be sent *from* heaven, but we are definitely sent *by* heaven. We may not be sent *across* a culture, but we are definitely sent *into* a culture. Our town is a culture, our schools have cultures, our neighborhoods have cultures, our activities—golfing, cycling, running, scrapbooking—can each have a culture of its own (often called a subculture). The culture where we live and/or spend significant portions of our time is often termed our "host culture."[74]

Virtually all of us reside in a host culture that is ignorant of, indifferent about, or hostile toward the gospel. As missionaries, our role is to understand the culture and attempt to enter it in every way we can, so the gospel may be introduced in a way that is both comprehensible and convicting. The goal is not to make the gospel palatable, but understandable; not to cover it, thus producing questionable conversions, but to unveil it, thus producing authentic ones.

Missional believers do not wait to be sent by a church or mission board into a foreign land, but recognize they are already sent from heaven to earth as Christ's messengers wherever they live, work, study, and play. Missional believers receive the call to participate in God's mission when answering the call to enter God's kingdom. All believers are missionaries to somebody, somewhere.

That includes us.

The world is not our home

Despite that call, observers of Western religious culture, perhaps especially American evangelicalism, would be hard pressed to believe that we view finances in the same way the average missionary is expected to do. Missionaries routinely sell their houses, cars, and furniture, fly far from home and live in a modest dwelling among the people they wish to impact for Christ. They drive a modest vehicle (often just one, sometimes provided by a mission board sometimes not), wear clothes appropriate to their new home and, generally, have enough money to live. Often their money is spent in ministry, especially if living in a less than affluent area. Though some missionaries engage in business, more often than not it is for the purpose of building relationships and may or may not be a profit-making venture. They typically view everything about their assignment as directly related to God's kingdom.

The contrast with American Christians could hardly be more stark. Most of us are multiple car families, have more house than we need, more stuff than we can use, make wasteful purchases without a second thought (much less prayer), and give 2.8 percent of our income to "charity," many of which have nothing to do with Kingdom purposes. Some Christians spend hundreds or thousands of dollars a year to enroll their kids in every manner of activity, far outpacing the amount given so the gospel can be taken to those who have never heard. Because we have so long believed that missionaries are "those super spiritual people who get sent to live with cannibals," and have failed to understand our own calling, it has been easy to excuse our lifestyles that might otherwise have been called exorbitant, wasteful, or excessive. When each believer begins to live as a sent messenger, a missionary on assignment, an ambassador in a foreign land, we can begin to more biblically evaluate our money and possessions.

Dr. Jerry Rankin is the president-emeritus of the International Mission Board of the Southern Baptist Convention. In his book, *Spiritual Warfare: The Battle for God's Glory*, he recounts two instances in which missionaries struggled with money or possessions. Of one, he writes: "A missionary, serving in a high-cost economy, resigned, explaining he could not possibly live on the support being provided...As an illustration of how they could not make it on their missionary salary, he pointed out that it cost his family $57 to eat out at McDonald's each week."[75] Another missionary struggled with the idea of moving to an area with no electricity or indoor plumbing. Rankin records, "A lady stood up in our meeting and spoke with emotion. With tears she said, 'We've got to do this. We've got to move to the villages and *kampungs* (neighborhood ghettos) if we're going to be used of God. We can't isolate ourselves and continue the way we've been living.' Then she blurted out between her sobs, 'But I can't give up my refrigerator!'"[76]

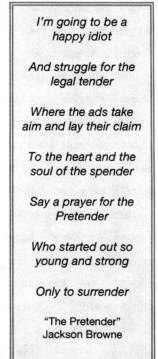

I'm going to be a happy idiot

And struggle for the legal tender

Where the ads take aim and lay their claim

To the heart and the soul of the spender

Say a prayer for the Pretender

Who started out so young and strong

Only to surrender

"The Pretender"
Jackson Browne

In our mind these stories might sound extreme. "How could a missionary be so concerned about this kind of thing? Are they not living in poor areas? Are they not expected to make sacrifices?" We might even laugh sympathetically at the lady's desire to have a refrigerator while we are grabbing a drink from our side-by-side LG with water and ice dispensers and, maybe, a built-in TV or computer screen. Are we guilty of judging in the midst of indulgence? James indicted his first century audience over this very issue, "You have lived luxuriously on the earth and led a life of wanton pleasure; you have fattened your hearts in a day of slaughter" (5:5; NASB).

Country, culture, context

The point we may miss is that each follower of Christ is a missionary in our country, our culture, and our context. There is not a single follower of Christ who is not called and sent. Should we judge that a missionary is not sufficiently in love with Christ when we do not give a second thought to vastly more wasteful expenditures than wanting to eat at McDonald's once a week? To tell some American Christians that they could only eat out once a week would be akin to putting them on the fast track to starvation since so many meals are eaten at restaurants. Years ago a young lady named Kirsten at the church where I was on staff had just returned from Papua New Guinea, or "PNG" as she called it. After two years of teaching children in the Wycliffe Bible Translators missionary school, she was sitting across my office and had this to say as she slowly shook her head, "I cannot believe how much money Americans spend going out to eat. If they only knew how much Kingdom work could be funded by that money."

A former pastor of mine, who answered the call to ministry after being married (and having three children), moved to Louisiana to attend seminary. His wife drove a school bus during their seminary years and he pastored a church (part-time) many miles from where they lived. I recall him telling many times that they would scrape and save every penny and nickel they could, putting the money in a jar. Then, once at year they would attire themselves, he in his best suit and she in her best dress, and go out to eat...at McDonald's.

Compare that with the attitude of the missionaries who felt somehow slighted because they could not eat out once a week. Now think about how much money Americans spend eating out; not out of necessity as when traveling away from home, but out of convenience. Some Christian businessmen eat breakfast, lunch and sometimes dinner at restaurants. Some pastors eat breakfast, lunch and sometimes dinner out at an exorbitant running cost.

The question for us should not be, "Can we not have what we like?" but "Can we not live with what we must and use the rest for the Kingdom?" The scripture says, "To whom much is given much is required,"[77] not "To whom much is given much is allowed." There seems to be no end to how much we can spend on things that bring us pleasure, while specifically ignoring the things that bring God pleasure. This is the result of materialism.

Remember the statistics from the introduction? Remember how much money is spent on pet stuff every year? Remember how much it costs to help all those male animals have better self-esteem through fake "parts"? Did you know that people in the United States and the European Union spend more than thirteen billion U.S. dollars annually on perfume and cologne?[78] Imagine how many children could be supported through Compassion International at thirty-four dollars a month with that surplus of redirected cash. (Save your imagination—it is 31,862,745 children.)

Scripture is not silent as to how we understand this earthly life: "Set your mind on things above, not on things on the earth."[79] "Do not lay up for yourselves treasures on earth."[80] "We are ambassadors for Christ."[81] "Do not be anxious about tomorrow."[82] Our problem is not that we have no access to the truth; the problem is that we have carefully censored the parts that make us uncomfortable. We are practicing revisionist missiology.

The worst-case scenario?

Actually, the problem may be worse than that. The worst-case scenario is that we have actually folded materialism into our worldview and are now unable to recognize it as such. Americans, for instance, have instilled within us from our earliest years that this is the "land of opportunity" where "each generation has done better than the one before it." Done better how? Morally? Philosophically? Spiritually? No, financially. Each generation has accumulated more stuff than the one preceding. This is expected; it is part of what it means to be an American. In fact, when the recent "Great Recession" wiped out so much paper and real estate wealth, the lament became that the next generation would be the first in our history not to have more than their parents.

> *I was young and I needed the money*
>
> *I had money, and I needed more money*
>
> *I was filthy rich-- all I wanted was love.*
>
> *And a little more money...*
>
> *Woe to you, proud mortal! secure in your modest digs*
>
> *You think you're immune?*
>
> "Cash Cow"
> Steve Taylor

The combination of the American Dream, the lack of understanding about each believer being a missionary, and the reality of God's universal ownership has birthed a generation of American believers who are blinded to their own materialistic worship. There is a very simple test that will demonstrate the kingdom to which we are aligned; ask yourself this: *When is the last time I had to forgo the purchase of anything at all, delay or cancel a vacation or cancel entertainment plans because my giving to the kingdom of God would not allow it?* The simple, but disheartening fact is that too often the opposite is true: we have often missed God-given opportunities due to our base worship of things. Before he reached the peak of his wealth, Andrew Carnegie wrote, "Man must have an idol—the amassing of wealth is one of the worst species of idolatry—no idol is more debasing than the worship of money."[83]

How our position as missionary relates to our use of possessions is only one side of the coin. The other side is that we are managers of portions of God's wealth as He distributes it.

A familiar tale

Years ago there lived a wealthy landowner who had an estate with numerous servants. Each of these servants had varying degrees of responsibility, which they performed for him at his command.

One day, the landowner's business carried him away for an extended period of time. He called some of his servants together for the purpose of giving them management responsibilities over certain segments of his possessions. To one of them he entrusted fifty thousand dollars, to another twenty thousand dollars, and to another ten thousand dollars; the decisions were made based on the management abilities that each had already demonstrated.

When the rich man left, the first two servants went to work in short order investing the money left in their care. Each was able to double the amount, the first to $100k, and the second to $40k. The third servant, however, took a different approach. He took the $10k entrusted to him, built a waterproof box, found a place on the back side of the property, dug a hole, and buried the box and money in the hole.

When the owner returned, he called the three servants, expecting an accounting for the money he had given. When the first two gave their reports, the owner was ecstatic. "Here," he said to the first, "you've done well. Now, experience my joy by taking authority over these ten cities!" The second servant received a similar commendation receiving responsibility over five cities.

The third servant then stood before the master who demanded to hear a report. "It's like this," the servant began, "when you gave me the money, I knew that you were a very forceful man, an austere boss. To tell you the truth, I was kind of afraid of what you would do if I didn't meet your expectations." Noticing the narrowing eyes of the master, the servant continued, stammering, "So, I t-took the entire $10k and b-buried it on the back of your property. Here it is, every p-penny!"

The master was visibly angry as he closed the short distance between he and the third servant until the faltering man had no personal space remaining at all. Almost nose-to-nose he finally spoke, "You are not just a foolish servant, you are a *wicked* man! You say that you knew I was a powerful, that I reap harvests that I had not sown. If you really believe that, the least you should have done was to have put the money in a CD at the bank and let it earn some interest! Do you not realize that inflation has actually made the money worth less than its value when I gave it to you?"

The master then stepped back a pace and yelled to some other servants standing by, "Take the box of money, open it and give it to the most successful servant. At least he knows how to properly invest my money. After you have done that, take this loser and throw him off my property forever. I don't care what happens to him, just get him away from me."[84]

Your cash ain't nothin'
but trash

Your cash ain't nothin'
but trash

Your cash ain't nothin'
but trash

But I'm sure gonna
get me some more

"Your Cash Ain't Nothin'
But Trash"
The Clovers

Those familiar with the New Testament may have noticed similarities to the parable of the talents taught by Jesus Christ. Despite the belief of some, this parable has nothing to do with abilities like playing piano, solving math problems, or hitting a baseball. The parable very specifically states the servants are managers of property and money. They are also judged by what kind of managers they each turn out to be. Two were well rewarded while one was judged and destroyed. This parable provides a great New Testament insight as to what God expects from His servants in relationship to what He owns.

The coming opportunity

This parable was given not long before Jesus was to return to the Father. His disciples would soon be given responsibilities they had only partially experienced while walking with Him. The unequivocal expectation God had for them was for faithful management; that expectation applies to us today. Everything we oversee by way of money and possessions is a test of faithfulness for us.[85] This faithfulness was (and is) to be exemplified by managing the investment opportunity in the way that the owner would were He here. How we manage God's possessions is a matter of faithfulness; how we give them is a matter of love.

Speaking of his denomination, a friend of mine likes to say, "There is only one pot of money and it's in the pockets of the people in the pews." It may sound simple, but that is true. It may come as a shock, but God has no bank account in your town. He has left a certain amount of wealth under the control of His children and that wealth is in bank accounts, stock accounts, safety deposit boxes, mattresses, Mason jars, goat pens, cow herds, and the hulls of ships worldwide. God's wealth resides in gold Maple Leafs, American Eagles, and Krugerrands; in silver and platinum bars, in collectible figurines, '65 Corvettes, pictures autographed by Jerry Garcia, and guitars that once belonged to Eric Clapton. He has wealth scattered everywhere under management of different people with different abilities. To those who have little, He expects faithfulness with little; from those who have much, He expects faithfulness with much. But do not be deceived; God expects faithfulness. As the Corinthians were reminded, "Now it is required that those who have been given a trust must prove faithful."[86] Alfred Edersheim, who was a scholar of 1st century Jewish culture, believed such mismanagement resulted from irresponsibility and a lack of effort. Writing of the wicked servant referenced above, he states, "The prominent fact here is, that he did not employ [the money] for the Master, as a good servant, but shunned alike the labor and the responsibility, and acted as if it has been some stranger's, and not his Lord's property."[87]

"Our" possessions are as much God's as if His name was on every deed and every single piece of ownership paperwork. "Our" money is also just as much at His disposal as if He had a debit card to our account and His name was on every check. Imagine checking your account online one morning to see that God had used His debit card to take three hungry people to IHOP the night before. What would you say? Would you complain about how God spent His money? Think it over: are we careful to spend our money the same way that God would? Spending the money God has entrusted to our management, without His involvement, is no different than embezzlement.

The shift

The authors of *A is for Abductive* issue this challenge:

It is also time for the church to ask its members some probing economic identity questions: Are you consumers? Are you citizens? Are you Christians?

If you are the first, your economics revolves around the question, Is this the best deal for me? If you are the second, your economics revolves around the question, Is this best for the nation? If you are the third, your economics revolves around a very different question, Is Christ calling me to do this?[88]

It will help us more easily accept our calling as missionary and our role as manager if we truly believe that God owns and sustains everything. It will also help to remember that God has taken upon Himself the responsibility to take care of His children. He has promised to provide for our needs; we are about to see that we can take Him at His word.

meditations

Using the following space, reflect on what Scripture impacted you the most in this chapter. What response does God require of you?

chapter five

God is bigger than my job

"And my God shall supply all of your needs, according to His riches in
glory in Christ Jesus."
Philippians 4:19 (NASB)

"Yet he commanded the skies above and opened the doors of heaven,
and he rained down on them manna to eat and gave them the grain of
heaven. Man ate of the bread of angels; he sent them food in
abundance."
Psalm 78: 22-25 (ESV)

If we think the goal of our finances is simply to pay cash for all our
purchases or to ensure we have a sufficient emergency fund, we can
lose touch with the fact that God, not budgeting, meets the needs of
our lives.

Time: Late 20s to early 30s AD, depending on whose calendar you read.

Place: The court at the Jewish temple, right beside the offering plates. (We can surmise they did not use buckets from the Hummus Hut.)

Participants: Jesus, His disciples, a bunch of rich people, a destitute widow.

The following is how this story might have been relayed before the inspired writers, Mark and Luke, penned their records.[89]

I made this up...obviously.

"Anybody seen the Lord in the last few minutes?" Peter asked the other eleven disciples.

"Not since He tied that last group of Pharisees in a knot," replied Andrew. The other disciples nodded their agreement as to the Lord's effectiveness in dealing with challengers. They shielded their eyes against the sun, deciding to wait until He made His way back to them.

Had they known where to find the Lord, they would have seen Him in the temple complex sitting over by the offering box, also called "the treasury." Since Jesus never did anything by accident, it was with purpose that He watched to see how the people gave.

"Hey, guys. Come over here a minute." The disciples could hear the voice of the Master over the shuffling and murmuring of the worshipers.

"Anybody see Him?" asked Thomas.

"I hear a voice, but I see no man," replied Andrew, bringing a head slap from someone behind him.

"Over here," came the voice of Jesus again. They looked to see His hand above the crowd and navigated toward Him.

"Is He over by the offering plates?" mused Thaddeus.

"Man, I hope this isn't another tithing sermon," said someone else who forever escaped identification. No one heard Judas say, under his breath, "I hope it is. My house payment is due."

The twelve men arrived beside Jesus. "What is it, Lord?" they wondered aloud.

"OK. I want you to watch this. You see all these people putting in their tithes and offerings?" He asked.

For the next few minutes they stood in silence as the worshipers filed by putting in their various amounts. Finally, Jesus said, "What do you see?"

They struggled to make any distinction. "Well," began Peter haltingly, "a lot of people are bringing their offerings and putting them in the treasury." He looked around for a little moral support from his compatriots. "Yeah," added Matthew, the former tax collector, "and some are putting in a LOT."

"Notice this," said Jesus. "Those you see putting in a lot of money also have a lot of money left over. Now, watch that widow."

They listened as the slightest tinkle of copper rattled against the money already in the box. With somewhat puzzled, sideways glances, the twelve semi-shrugged their shoulders as they tried to figure out the Master's point.

"It might not have looked like much," the Lord resumed His teaching, "but those two coins were all that she had. It was her entire living in this world." Looking slowly from face to face He finally said, "She gave more than any of the others."

A matter of perspective

The historical record of Jesus and the widow's mites is outstanding in its simplicity. The widow gave all that she had—two copper coins worth less than almost nothing. We are given nothing about her history and the Lord tells us nothing of her future. The only insight we are given into her life is this single act and, like the woman who washed and anointed Jesus feet, this sacrificial act has been a memorial to her since.

What we *are* told in this story is the evaluation that God gave regarding her gift. In God's economy, this "pauper widow"[90] gave more than all the others who contributed. As a result, it becomes clear the "how" of their giving for which Jesus watched: a percentage of the whole. He was interested to see not what was given, but what was kept. In the case of the crowds, much was kept; in the case of the widow, nothing was kept.

If this was anyone other than Jesus Christ as the point man in this story we might think them prone to hyperbole, just an exaggeration to make a point. But for Jesus not only to say it, but to doubly emphasize it ("out of her poverty", "all she had to live on") is no teacher's ploy. The widow literally had nothing left. Paul described the giving of Macedonian believers in a similar way, "Out of their extreme poverty, they abounded in generosity."

Randy Alcorn makes an interesting observation[91] about how we might respond in a situation similar to the widow's coins. If a widow in our church came to the offering plate with everything that she had, we

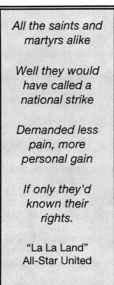

All the saints and martyrs alike

Well they would have called a national strike

Demanded less pain, more personal gain

If only they'd known their rights.

"La La Land"
All-Star United

would likely try to talk her out of giving it based on her extreme need. But Jesus did not do this. He knew that His Father would bless this woman's obedience and used her sacrifice as an example to us all. When it comes to missional giving, we cannot compare what we are accustomed to giving with what God might require in a specific opportunity. His call for financial sacrifice is not likely to make sense to our materially satiated Western appetites.

God's beating heart

Without a doubt God has a special spot in His heart for widows. Multiple times in the Law of Moses we read of God's design to make sure that widows have their needs met or are otherwise protected. In Exodus 22:22-24, God said, "You shall not afflict any widow or fatherless child. If you afflict them in any way, and they cry at all to Me, I will surely hear their cry; and my wrath will become hot and I will kill you with the sword; your wives shall become widows, and your children fatherless" (NKJV). God's retribution on those who destroyed widows was to put their own wives in the same situation. In the second giving of the law, God said, "The Lord your God is God of gods and Lord of lords, the great God, mighty and awesome, who shows no partiality nor takes a bribe. He administers justice for the fatherless and the widow, and loves the stranger, giving him food and clothing" (Deut. 10:17, 18; NKJV).

Perhaps the most poignant, prophetic love story in the Old Testament is in the book of Ruth. God provided for Ruth and Naomi, her mother-in-law, through a near relative who adhered to a specific part of the law given so the needs of the widows in Israel might be met (Deut. 24, 29-21). At a different time, when harsh judgment was being announced on both Israel and Judah, God's repeated warnings through the prophets were focused on lack of justice, including the mistreatment of widows. Isaiah, Jeremiah, Ezekiel, Zechariah, and Malachi[92] all contain prophecies of God's anger with the people and their leaders. David wrote that God, "in His holy Habitation," is a "defender of widows" (Ps. 68:5; NKJV).

It really should not surprise anyone that when God wanted to give an example of missional giving, He used a widow. And when He wanted to use powerful demonstrations of His ability to provide, He used a widow.

The sky is falling!

We are introduced to the prophet Elijah as abruptly as a safe falling from ten floors up onto the sidewalk in front of us. No mending nets with his father or sitting under a fig tree for Elijah. He springs onto the pages of Scripture fully formed in the throes of prophetic warning: "As the Lord God of Israel lives, before whom I stand, there shall not be dew nor rain these years, except at my word" (1 Kings 17:1; NKJV). Well, "top o' the morning to you, Elijah." I can only imagine how the king's press secretary was hustling to spin that particular pronouncement.

We are told that Elijah is a Tishbite from Gilead and that he is speaking to the vile, wicked, pathetic king Ahab of Israel. Scripture records in the verses immediately preceding that "Ahab the son of Omri did evil in the sight of the Lord, more than all who were before him." Further, he married the woman whose name has forever since described vile, despicable, ungodly women: Jezebel. Ahab built a temple to her god, Baal, in Samaria, even worshiping this false god himself. He also built an Ashera pole[93] for worship as if God's people needed any more encouragement to turn from Him. Had Ahab known the ultimate severity of the drought—it lasted more than three years—he might have fired up a chainsaw himself and done some pole-cutting.

I don't know what they want from me

It's like the more money we come across

The more problems we see

Mo' Money, Mo' Problems
The Notorious B.I.G.

Dry, dry, and more dry

Summers with little rain are not uncommon where I live in Georgia. In the past decade we have experienced two separate droughts that saw lake levels drop to dangerously low levels and four Southern states involved in intramural squabbles about water supplies. Many trees and bushes used in southern planting have been bred to be drought resistant, but week after week of scorching sun and little rain leads to the death of much plant life. These periods of drought have come with their attendant warnings that it will take twenty years to return to normal water levels (it never took that long). Thankfully, we have never experienced three years with neither rain nor dew!

After Elijah delivered his warning, God immediately removed him from Samaria into the wilderness where ravens brought his daily meals and his water supply was provided by the brook Cherith, east of the Jordan River. As is the normal result of a drought, the brook that supplied Elijah's needs eventually turned to dust. So that Elijah would not be left "high and dry," so to speak, God gave the prophet instructions to travel to Zarephath, where He had commanded a widow to make provision for him. Zarephath (Sarepta) was outside Israel, being located in a narrow plain between the range of Lebanon and the Mediterranean Sea.[94]

Upon entering the city, Elijah found the designated widow collecting sticks for a fire. Doubtless parched and hungry after the walk, he asked for some water and bread. She responded, "As the Lord your God lives, I have nothing baked, only a handful of flour in a jar and a little oil in a jug. When I finish gathering these sticks, I'm going to cook a little something for myself and my son, then we will wait to die."[95] This is a pretty sad tale, like something from Cormac McCarthy's book, The Road, or the Denzel Washington movie, The Book of Eli. At this point Elijah makes what must seem, to any reasonable bystander, an absurdly selfish request: "That's cool. Do just what you've said. But before you cook that last loaf of bread for yourself and your son, make a cake for me. Then make something for yourself and your son." In other words, "I know you're starving to death and all, but give me your last morsel of food first."

And we wonder why preachers have such bad reputations!

The reality behind this self-serving statement was that God was using Elijah's request to test her faith. If God had already commanded her to provide for Elijah, then this was the last hurdle she had to pass through before God intervened on her behalf and enabled her to do so. This became clear as Elijah continued, "For thus says the Lord the God of Israel, 'The jar of flour shall not be spent, and the jug of oil shall not be empty, until the day that the Lord sends rain upon the earth.'"[96] The Bible further records that she, her son and Elijah lived for many days from the never emptying jar and jug. As Matthew Henry notes, "One poor meal's meat this poor widow gave the prophet, and, in recompense of it, *she and her son did eat many days* (v. 15), above two years, in a time of general scarcity."[97]

This miracle is an instance of the owner (God) redirecting His supplies to bless an anonymous widow and her son. The widow had undoubtedly seen others die; from her conversation it is obvious she had come to expect it herself. Few, if any, are the famines that do not see death in great and terrible numbers.[98] In His grace, God had other plans for her. In response to her obedience and faith, she and her son were able to experience the power of God in a magnificent way and bless a weary prophet as well. This blessing was returned unexpectedly after the boy contracted an unidentified illness and died. In an action unprecedented in biblical history, Elijah stretched himself atop the corpse three times while crying out to God for a miracle. God heard Elijah's prayer and revived the boy.[99] So, God thus supplied not only her immediate physical needs, but restored the one whose responsibility it would be to meet her future needs. Thankfully, God did not stop meeting needs when Elijah left this place with a whirlwind fueling his chariot of fire.[100]

Back to the beginning

A few years into our marriage I became incapacitated and unable to work. Wow, is *that* an understatement. Allow me to skip back a few songs...

When we first married, we made a commitment that Sonya would work until we had kids, then she would exit the job place and be a fulltime homemaker. After two whole months of wedded bliss, she was found to be with child and it was not of the Holy Spirit. Quite apart from our master plan she was going to be exiting the work force after less than one year of marriage. This was after I had already asked my boss for a raise from $6.00/hr to $6.50/hr just so I could get married in the first place.

A budding Bill Gates I was not.

Despite the fact that she accounted for about one-third of our small income, we were determined to be obedient to what we believed God was leading us to do. One day on the job, I struck up a conversation with a homeowner where I was working. He was a delivery service owner that subcontracted with a major overnight package carrier. As a result of that conversation, I left my initial employer for his delivery company. I started the week that Sonya left her job and enjoyed an increase in salary that compensated for our loss of income. In addition, I would have increases in responsibility and salary that I would never have had.

After about a year, I suffered a career-ending knee injury. No, not the delivery career—my Sunday afternoon, after church, tackle football career. Playing with a bunch of church guys, I went out for a pass from the wide receiver position. It was a play I had run a thousand times since I was a kid, but this time when I made the out cut, my left knee made an in cut. The not-so-pleasant result was a torn medial-collateral ligament, anterior-cruciate ligament, and a rupture of the capsule surrounding the knee joint. It was a college or pro level knee injury. Not such a good idea for a man who walked miles every day delivering overnight packages.

I'm sure everyone in my family saw job loss and moving in with parents as the new next step in the master plan, but it never crossed my mind. I had a scalpel to deal with. And IVs. And shots. I approached the impending surgery like Captain Kirk had just said, "Set phasers to stun."

> *Left a good job in the city*
>
> *Working for the man every night and day*
>
> *And I never lost one minute of sleeping*
>
> *Worrying about the way things might have been*
>
> "Proud Mary"
> Creedence Clearwater Revival

While still in the hospital recovering, my boss stopped by to see how I was doing. To my surprise, he dropped my paycheck on my bed and said, "Don't worry." I didn't, and he paid my salary through my extensive physical therapy and months of limited working ability. He was not a believer, but God used him to meet our needs at a time when we were still a young family with a small daughter. In a strange way he was Pharaoh to my Joseph.

Fool me once...

Over the next few years, another of our employees had severe enough injuries away from the job that a new company policy had to be instituted: Any injuries sustained off the job (especially related to playing sports) would result in the loss of employment. It was very clear that hyperbole was not the order of the day. The boss meant what he said.

So....

I had given up Sunday afternoon *football* for Sunday afternoon *basketball*. So much less stress on the knees and all that. Since my orthopedic doctor has prescribed a Lenox Hill knee brace for me ("The same kind Joe Namath had," he said), I thought I was safe. Chasing down a loose ball, however, I suddenly felt a strange pain in my other knee. Not quite as damaging as before, but I was facing surgery again; and missing more work.

My boss knew I had injured my knee again, but was willing to wait for the diagnosis. I was a good employee and he wanted to make sure it was not merely a sprain. When the morning of the great summit arrived, the news was broken that I was facing yet another knee surgery with a loss of time. My boss looked at me and said, "Marty, I've already talked to the workman's comp people and told them you may have injured your knee while you were out on the dock working. I could file with them and we could probably save your job."

Now my boss had known virtually since the first day that I was a believer, and knew I tried to live that faithfully across all phases of the job. I also knew what would happen if I acquiesced to his suggestion. A smile came across my face. "Boss," I said, "I really, really appreciate what you are trying to do. But you know I cannot do that." He half smiled and said, "I know, but I thought I'd throw it out there." I left without the job but with testimony intact.

Of glue guns and God

Sonya's creative streak had really blossomed during the time she had been home with our daughter. Specifically, she had learned to make all kinds of decorative craft items for people's houses. She had participated in one or two craft fairs and done well; besides that, it was something she really enjoyed.

Remember that part in the story about being incapacitated and unable to work? For the second time in the first five years of our marriage I was unable to work, had a full leg-length cast and, this time, out of a job. With no other options, I went through on-the-job-training on how to use a hot glue gun, cut plastic flowers, spray paint wicker baskets, and other things that would hurt my masculinity if I were to confess them.

It was during this time that we first truly learned about God's ability to provide for us and His willingness to do so. Our pastor had always been faithful to teach our church about giving, even having stewardship revivals with preachers who taught from Scripture about trusting God to meet our needs. Some of the stories were incredible, straining the edges of credulity for this newly married couple.

I remember a moment of frustration, probably owing as much to my Percocet prescription as not, that Sonya said, "You know, I think those guys just make up those stories. Do you think that God really does that for them?" We were talking around our makeshift workbench (a broken ping-pong table) not long after my surgery, facing an immeasurable uphill struggle to pay bills by selling wall hangings, table décor, and knick-knacks. No Fortune 500 companies were beating down our door.

At this point, we took the biggest step of faith we had experienced since bringing our daughter home from the hospital as two too young parents. We decided to give 20 percent of our "profits" as our regular offering. We had no unemployment income, no other salary, no stock dividends, and no derivatives. Our logic was impeccable: We are going to starve to death anyway, we might as well give as much as we can and see if God will be good to His word. Did I say "impeccable"?

*The pusher push,
the fixer fix
the judge acquits*

*The junkie leads his life
for the dollar bill
funky dollar bill
funky dollar bill
U.S. dollar bill*

"Funky Dollar Bill"
George Clinton and the
Funkadelics

Before long, God began to provide through more different avenues than we could count. Every time we took crafts to a retail shop, they paid exactly what we were asking without batting an eye. Every craft show was a success; we only did Saturday shows, reserving Sunday for the Lord's Day. God seemed to give us two days worth of sales every time. We received anonymous offerings. On two different occasions I found money in our car, once the exact amount of our rent when it was a few days past due.

One day we received a phone call from a friend. "We just bought some beef from the butcher and they cut too much of it into ground beef. We don't eat that much ground beef. Can we bring you some?" "Sure." Really, what else are we going to say? Later that day, she pulled into our driveway with ground beef, steaks, roasts, and whatever else you can cut off a cow not counting the horns and udders. Another time she called and said, "My dad works at a company with a big, big food pantry. Can I bring you some food from that?" "Sure." This far along we do not remember all she brought, but one thing has always stuck out: Cocoa Pebbles. We had so many boxes of Cocoa Pebbles that our cabinets *and freezer* were full of them. There were some days that we ate Cocoa Pebbles for two meals a day! The funny thing is we never, ever got tired of them and like them to this day.

When God promised to meet our needs, I do not think He specified a great variety, necessarily. The children of Israel had manna, manna, manna, then quail, quail, quail. It seems, "Don't talk with your mouth full," as our parents always said, is applicable here.

God supplied our needs for months, from around February to July of that year, with neither of us having a regular job. Then, suddenly, like Elijah's stream, the supply started to dry up. We did not really know all of what was happening, but we believed that God was about to move us in another direction; that He did. One day I received a phone call from the president of a Bible college I had attended. He was doing an interim pastorate and wanted to recommend me to the church. By the end of July, I had accepted the pastorate, moved into the pastorium (parsonage) and started receiving a fulltime salary again. During this entire turn of events God always met every need that we had.

There are many, many more stories that could be told from our experiences with God's provision, from expenses for mission trips, an unexpected check to finish work on our house that was within one dollar of what we needed, to college expenses always being covered. How we came to trust God's provision was a learning process; a process based in Scripture.

One of the most important instances of provision in the entire Scripture was a ram provided for Abraham in place of the son, Isaac. Following the call of God to sacrifice his son as an offering, the father of faith stood with knife held high over Isaac ready at any moment to plunge it into his heart. It was at this fail-safe moment when God revealed this to be only a test, that Abraham spied God's intended victim: a ram caught in a thicket. Abraham renamed the mountain where this drama took place, "The Lord will provide," a confirmation of his earlier declaration of faith, "God will provide for himself the lamb for a burnt offering, my son" (Gen. 22:8, 14; ESV). Referring to the underlying Hebrew Old Testament text, Nelson writes, "What we learn from Genesis 22:8 and 14 is that God is both 'the God who sees and who will "see to it.'"[101] When God "sees" the need of His child, He "sees to" meeting that need.

God just knows how

Prior to the provision for Elijah and the widow of Zarephath, God provided daily for dietary needs of wandering Israelites whose number surely exceeded a million people, then later for more than five thousand in a crowd of Jesus' listeners, for Paul in ministry and for Jewish believers in Jerusalem. In each biblical study my wife and I could find, God provided for the needs of His people. We became convinced that God could provide for us as well.

During those days of job loss and craft fairs, we never prayed specifically for Cocoa Pebbles (who would?) or ground beef. We only asked that God would show Himself strong for us and provide for our needs and believed that He would do so. I wonder sometimes if what we timidly call "faith" is more often "fate" instead. Some expect God to intervene without asking Him for His aid, while others never consider the possibility of His action on behalf of His children. I believe completely in God's absolute sovereignty, but this does not mean that we are locked out of participating in the world He has created. The late pastor William E. Sangster addressed this when he said,

"It may be felt...that no room has been left in the scheme of things for any 'special' Providence at all. It will appear to some that if we are not pawns of chance we are prisoners of law, and they will wonder if half our petitions are not a waste of time.

"Yet that would be a sad and false conclusion, and one unwarranted by the facts. If the relationship between God and His human children is best conceived as that of Father and child, it may safely be assumed that God has not so made the world that He cannot make a Father's response to a child's plea."[102]

This is true, of course, and one of the reasons we are encouraged to pray. We have no reason to believe that God is no longer looking the world over to show Himself strong for those whose hearts are completely His![103] When we act in faith, God responds.

OK, God can meet my needs, now what?

Understanding God's power to provide is a major step in the life of every believer. Those who have not learned this have only the deep insecurity brought by trusting things for security. Possessions cannot bring safety because it is not in their nature to do so. Assurance of

God's provision does more than give us security for our groceries; it is the ground of faith for missional giving.

meditations

Using the following space, reflect on what Scripture impacted you the most in this chapter. What response does God require of you?

chapter six

becoming missional givers

"Out of the most severe trial, their overflowing joy and their extreme
poverty welled up in rich generosity."
2 Corinthians 8:2 (NIV)

"See that you also excel in this grace of giving."
2 Corinthians 8:7 (NIV)

You want to know what's wrong with our waterfront? It's the love of
a lousy buck. It's love of a buck, the cushy job, more important than
the love of man!
Father Barry (Karl Malden)
On the Waterfront

I am not by nature a generous person. I'm more what you might call, "generous by degrees." I tend to be fairly generous with some things, but not so generous with others. For instance, I'm OK with giving money to someone who lost a job, buying Christmas presents for kids who are not going to have gifts on the 25th of December, giving an offering for a guest speaker, or a family who lost everything in a house fire. On the other hand, **do not** ask me for a SweeTart; that's where I draw the line. I'm not likely to share a Snickers with you either. There are some things I'm just not sure God would ask this child to do.

A couple of years ago, I was invited to speak to a group of pastors in Oklahoma. The leader who invited me, John, picked me up at the airport and we started a multi-hour ride back to the city where the event would be hosted. Pretty quickly he noticed my roll of SweeTarts and mentioned his affinity for, I believe, the blue ones. It grieved me to no end that he was worming his way into my candy stash. It was only with the greatest personal suffering that he received a few of those tantalizing discs of Dextrose, Maltodextrin, Malic Acid, Calcium Stearate, artificial flavors, Blue 1 Lake, Blue 2 Lake, Red 40 Lake, Yellow 5 Lake, and Yellow 6 Lake.

I mean, c'mon. I would have bought him an apple.

This is not to say I have never known moments of generosity. As a teenager holding my first job, our church went to a Bible conference known for spontaneous times of generosity called "giving services."

People would commit money with reckless abandon, often with no prompting from the pastor or for any specific reason. One person might stand and say, "God is prompting me to give a hundred dollars," while another person might donate material items: shoes, art, or a car.

> I'll give you all I got to give
> if you say you love me too
>
> I may not have a lot to give
> but what I got I'll give to
> you
>
> I don't care too much for
> money
> money can't buy me love
>
> "Can't Buy Me Love"
> The Beatles

Often when non-cash items were given, a second person would offer cash to "redeem" the item back to its owner. This saved the camp from having to take the time to sell all the items.

It was during one of these services that a painting called "The Seventh Day" was offered. It was one artist's conception of the day God rested and was, ostensibly, his idea of what Eden looked like immediately after creation. I had just received my income tax return and was flush with all the cash a teen could hope to have at once. Believing I was prompted by the Holy Spirit, I stood and offered five hundred dollars for the artwork. I have it until this day.

On another occasion after I accepted Christ, God seemed to be leading me to give some things I had accumulated. One item a very nice pair of boots that I had purchased during a phase then worn once or twice. These were given to a friend at church who liked boots. Another thing was a very nice, very expensive radio-controlled Corvette, which would run up to 30 mph (actual speed, not scale). I gave it to different church friend who liked electronics. Around this same time I also took from the cash I had on hand and purchased a suit for my Father and, I believe, some clothes for my Mother.

But for every time I have given joyfully from my possessions there have been others that I gave grudgingly or not at all. It is an ongoing battle. While The Arcade Fire may have overstated their case in their song, "City With No Children," the waffling generosity described seems unusually apt for me: *You never trust a millionaire quoting the Sermon on the Mount. I used to think I was not like them, but I'm beginning to have my doubts, my doubts about it.*

An anchor text for missional giving

Second Corinthians chapters 8 and 9 can form an anchor teaching for what it means to be a missional giver. As the text unfolds, the missionary/preacher known as the Paul, the Apostle to the Gentiles, is reminding the believers in the ancient city of Corinth of an offering for needy saints in Judea. It was an offering he had previously mentioned to them and for which they were supposed to be preparing themselves. Paul himself would not be coming to receive the money; he would be sending a team led by Titus.[104] Paul encouraged the Corinthian believers to prepare the offering ahead of time so that it would be obvious their giving was both planned and willful. He did not want it to look as if he had browbeaten them into submission.

In order to challenge them to a sacrificial level of giving, the apostle introduced the Corinthians to the Macedonians who were believers in another part of the Roman Empire. Macedonia, which included the biblical cities of Berea, Philippi and Thessalonica, had once been a wealthy region but had fallen on hard times after the Romans took control of the gold and silver mines. The ensuing poverty was extreme, described by the Greek word *ptocheia*, which denotes abject poverty; that which has literally nothing. The people were in imminent danger of real starvation. There were many poor people in the Roman Empire due, in part, to high taxes, high rent and high food prices. As if this was not bad enough, it was worse for followers of Christ. Neil Cole adds, "During a time of prevalent emperor worship, it was common for Christians to be virtually unemployable in the marketplace."[105]

This passage is the longest continuous teaching on giving in the New Testament. Drawing from the examples of the Macedonians and Corinthians, a biblical foundation is formed for missional giving. Upon this foundation, missionary managers, with the Spirit's power, can align their money and possessions with the activity of the King.

Missional giving is empowered by grace[106]

Six times in 2 Corinthians 8 and 9 the word *grace* is used in conjunction with financial giving. This sacrificial, beyond all means giving has for years been called "grace giving" by preachers and teachers. However, I believe the better understanding is that missional giving is empowered by grace. The Corinthian believers are called upon to "excel in this grace." It is grace that empowers the Macedonians to give out of their poverty and grace that empowers the Corinthians to give from their plenty. When our giving is empowered by grace, as with salvation, boasting has no place to stand.

It is grace that justifies, grace that glorifies, and grace that sanctifies. The attitudinal journey from owner to manager is part of the sanctification process and is smothered in the undeserved goodness of God. The further step of giving as Jesus and Paul commend is also empowered by God's grace. Missional giving is not birthed from my own "can do" attitude, but is a humble participation in God's mission.

Missional giving is expressed by generosity[107]

Twice Paul commended churches for their generosity, the church at Corinth and the churches of Macedonia. Though both were giving to the same offering, the former were giving from a position of relative financial strength (8:14), while the latter were giving out of a dearth of resources. He described the condition of the Macedonian churches as "extreme poverty" in "a test of severe affliction" (2

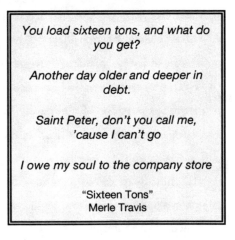

You load sixteen tons, and what do you get?

Another day older and deeper in debt.

Saint Peter, don't you call me, 'cause I can't go

I owe my soul to the company store

"Sixteen Tons"
Merle Travis

Cor. 8:2; ESV). The giving, however, is described as "a wealth of generosity." Like the widows discussed earlier, these destitute believers gave much more than they should have been judged able. This is exactly how Paul described it to the Corinthians, "they gave according to their means and beyond their means." We are not told the specifics of how they were able to do this, only that God graced them to do so (2 Cor. 8:1).

Generosity almost always requires that we give more than we think we should or can. It rarely means that we pull out all our bank statements, reconcile the books and make a decision based on asset liquidity. Generosity can only be a reality in our lives when we learn to hold things with a loose grip so they are *always* available for Kingdom purposes. As C.S. Lewis wrote, "The measure of a life, after all, is not its duration, but its donation."[108]

It should not be surprising if most believers struggle with generosity; it would, after all, fit with the writings of the New Testament. Paul warned about the dangers of wealth accumulation and provided the antidote. The rich are to set their hopes on God rather than their riches; be rich in good works, not only money; and, be generous and ready to share.[109] Regarding this text, Blomberg writes, "A key to preventing material possessions from becoming an idol is to give generous portions of them away. Our heavenly reward will more than compensate for what is 'lost' in the process."[110] While Blomberg calls giving "a key" to battling materialism, I believe generosity is the singular best way to consistently dethrone mammon. Materialism cannot maintain a hold on us if we are always giving away the substance of its godhood. When we continuously reject possessions as master, they return to the proper status as tools in God's kingdom.

Missional giving is generated from freedom[111]

Remember all those televangelists weeping for us to "Send money or fifteen television stations are going off the air!!"? What about those pleas from other leaders about bills that need to be paid, mansions that need maintenance, jets that need fuel or miracles that God is just waiting to send your way? How many times have believers written checks out of guilt (or felt guilty for not writing the check) not really hyped up about the "need" in the first place? The New Testament warns against this very kind of high pressure, veins and eyes bulging, sky is falling kind of manipulation.

There could scarcely be a greater need than to help those in a famine, yet Paul says of their offering, "I am not saying this as a command" (2 Cor. 8:8; HCSB). Later he says, "Don't give reluctantly or in response to pressure" (2 Cor. 9:7; NLT). Giving under guilt or pressure takes away the joy of giving. The opportunity itself should be all the "need" a missional giver needs.

Missional giving is accompanied by joy[112]

The Macedonians were in the throes of financial crisis. To juxtapose two adjectives, these believers had a wealth of poverty. The only thing they had plenty of was nothing. They were not being asked to appear on CNBC's *Squawk Box* to offer financial advice. They knew firsthand what Groucho Marx humorously described in *Monkey Business*, "Oh, I know it's a penny here and a penny there, but look at me. I worked myself up from nothing to a state of extreme poverty." In spite of this, when the Macedonians found out about the saints in need, they begged Paul and the others to allow them to participate in that ministry opportunity! No excuses, no hand wringing, not even a good old, "That sounds awful. I wish I could help, but I don't have anything myself." They pleaded with Paul to allow their involvement.

This joy is a prelude to the better known phrase, "God loves a cheerful giver" (9:7). The word from the original language indicates *hilarity*; exuberant joy. This joy comes from a heart abandoned to God; a heart not burdened by the idolatry of mammon. A primary reason so many have so little joy in giving is because they are giving their god away. When the Lord is God, giving is part and parcel of walking with Him. When mammon is on the throne and we are forced to part with it, there is severe separation anxiety. Those who serve Jesus are brought closer through missional giving; those who serve mammon worry over the absence of their god.

Missional giving is guided by purpose[113]

Craig Blomberg believes this offering was a "relief offering" for

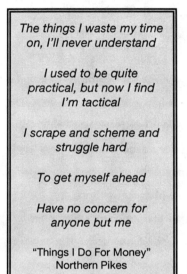

The things I waste my time on, I'll never understand

I used to be quite practical, but now I find I'm tactical

I scrape and scheme and struggle hard

To get myself ahead

Have no concern for anyone but me

"Things I Do For Money"
Northern Pikes

believers victimized by a famine which scourged Judea. Prophesied by Agabus in Acts 11,[114] the dearth reached its worst around 46 AD. This offering would be guided toward those still suffering in the famine's aftermath.[115]

Missional giving does not prefer a scattershot approach to biblical stewardship; it takes a guided, purposeful approach looking for needs and opportunities that will bear Kingdom fruit. This Macedonian/Corinthian offering was not a "missions offering," as twenty-first century American believers would think about it, but it was an offering in support of the mission of God, part of which is ministry *to* saints *by* saints.

There is also a tendency among missional givers to eschew giving toward wasteful, poorly managed, or inefficient organizations. Believers will be judged according to how we manage the resources God has entrusted to us. As a result, missional givers look for opportunities where the result is not inhibited by waste. The theme of the parables is that God is displeased with those servants who act wickedly, who mismanage resources or who are wasteful. Organizations that have become the end rather than the means make poor Kingdom investments.

Missional giving is relational before financial[116]

Paul writes that this type of giving was to God first and then to his team. This giving was not simply about the money; the Macedonian gifts to the Judeans in need was a result of giving themselves to God and to the ministry. Our relationship with God precedes (and should compel) our financial obedience. The actual giving, though, brings more joy and more satisfaction when a relationship exists between giver and receiver. (Not to mention importance of accountability.) This aspect of missional giving is based in community. The motivation to give springs from the relationships involved—what was important to God and Paul was important to the Macedonians and it was this relationship Paul hoped would help motivate the Corinthians to missional giving.

This communal aspect has been experienced by believers in churches for years. When a pastor or missionary is sent out from a local body, there is a much closer tie than when there is only an organizational relationship. Needs are much more quickly understood and have more thorough responses when the persons are known, or, in the case of Paul, the go-between is well known by both parties.

My parents are both retired and living on a modest income. Recently they decided, for the first time, to track their expenses by going on a budget. My sister and I spent a few hours reviewing their finances and then sat down with pencil and paper for a few more hours' work. It was during this process that my parents demonstrated they are indeed missional givers.

Mom and Dad have supported various missionaries since I was a child; most of them we had in our home and our church at one time or another. By now I would guess some of those ministries had been blessed by their consistent love gifts for more than three decades, gifts which continued as my parents passed from the "income earner" status to "fixed income" status.

After finishing the budget process, having squeezed every nickel dry, I looked at my parents and said, "OK, here's what you need to understand. At this point, to increase your spendable income you have two choices: either increase your income or cut your giving somewhere." They both realized I would never suggest they stop giving to their local church and understood I meant the extra giving to the missionaries and ministries they had long supported. Almost at the same time, they said, "We aren't cutting our giving." The sustained relationships they enjoyed meant more to them than the money did. Each of them had given themselves to God and to those in need.

Missional giving is a test of love[117]

Paul did not play the "Apostle card" on them as he had earlier in his first letter. He did not want them to give simply because he was encouraging them to do so. They needed to express their love through offerings. The principle Paul was instilling in them was much more important than handing down an Apostolic cyclical demanding twelve baskets of wheat from every person. By establishing generous giving as the test of true love, Paul set a measure that would last beyond his ministry with them and indeed his lifespan. As such, missional giving is a test of our love. If our giving is a reflection of our love toward God and His kingdom, where would we rate on the "Love-O-Meter"? Explosive? On Fire? Molten? Cold? Clammy? Sad? Perhaps worst of all: Lukewarm.[118]

The apostle John wrote to a group of young believers about the potential objects of our love. "Do not love the world or the things in the world. If anyone loves the world, the love of the Father is not in him. For all that is in the world—the lust of the flesh, the lust of the eyes and the pride of life—is not of the Father but is of the world."[119] The opportunity to give is a test of love; it is a test of who we love more, Jesus or the world, God or mammon.

Missional giving is rewarded proportionately[120]

Though not always portrayed in the same words, there is a sowing and reaping principle throughout the Bible that has to do with giving; it is not isolated to the church at Corinth. The writer in Proverbs observed, "There is one who scatters, yet increases more; and there is one who withholds more than is right, but it leads to poverty" (Prov. 11:24; NKJV). The psalmist wrote, referring to a righteous person, "He has distributed freely; he has given to the poor; his righteousness endures forever; his horn is exalted in honor" (Ps. 112:9; ESV). Another verse serves as a forerunner to the action of the Macedonians, "One who is gracious to a poor man lends to the Lord, and He will repay him for his good deed" (Prov. 19:17; NASB). The Lord Jesus said, "Give, and it will be given to you. Good measure, pressed down, shaken together, running over, will be put into your lap. For with the same measure you use it will be measured back to you" (Luke 6:38; ESV). Paul's word to the Corinthians regarding their

giving opportunity was that whoever sowed sparingly would reap
sparingly, and whoever sowed bountifully would reap bountifully.

Suppose in the spring you decided to plant some corn. Off to the
Feed and Seed you go and pick up a fifty-pound bag of seed. Back at
the farm (or the backyard), you begin to fret: "How much corn will I
get?" The answer, really, is in how much seed you plant. If you plant a
little, you will harvest a little. If you plant all fifty pounds, you will
harvest a lot—enough to feed the family, give some to friends and
possibly sell some as well. Ken Hemphill sees an Old Testament
corollary in Hosea 10:12, "Sow righteousness for yourselves and reap
faithful love; break up your untilled ground. It is time to seek the Lord
until He comes and sends righteousness on you like rain." He then
notes, "God's purpose in providing and multiplying our seed is not to
make us wealthy but to give us a fruitful ministry of righteousness."[121]

Hemphill touches on a key that is often overlooked. The reaping is
a reaping of righteousness, not necessarily money. This is because in
the economy of God, the financial act is qualified by its righteousness.
This is seen in Paul's use of Ps. 112:9 ("He has distributed freely, he
has given to the poor; his righteousness endures forever") and his tie-
in that sowing would "increase the harvest of [their] righteousness."[122]
The sowing of a small righteous act reaps a small harvest; the sowing
of a generous righteous act reaps a big harvest. The great benefit to us
is that we do not always know where the harvest will spring up. In the
life of one, it might be children who are given great influence in
Kingdom things, in another it may be an exemplary marriage that
models Christ and the church for all to see, in yet another it might be
increased financial responsibilities and opportunities for supporting

God's work. Scripture says, "You will be enriched *in every way* for all your generosity."[123]

Missional giving is sensitive to opportunity[124]

Pride tricks us into believing that we are generous because we give when we feel good doing so, but the New Testament connects

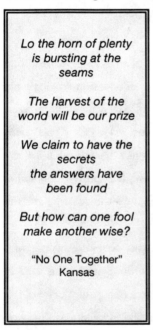

Lo the horn of plenty
is bursting at the
seams

The harvest of the
world will be our prize

We claim to have the
secrets
the answers have
been found

But how can one fool
make another wise?

"No One Together"
Kansas

generosity to giving when we have opportunity. A number of years ago, I had saved up some money to purchase something I wanted. Or maybe it was just something I was getting ready to want, I cannot remember specifically. It was nearing Christmas and a young, single mom we knew came across my mind. She had two little kids; I could only imagine how she was going to be able to buy anything for them. God put on my heart the money I had set aside, so I gave it all to her for Christmas. Later, she wrote me this note: "As soon as you gave me the $$ I was thankful, but when it turned out to be exactly the amount I needed to buy all the kids Christmas and pay off my daycare, I was thrilled!...God's timing could not have been better! Thank you for letting God use you to teach me a lesson about trusting Him."[125]

Missional giving is about being ready to give when opportunities arise. Whether a neighbor who needs groceries, a missionary who needs support, some kids who need Christmas, or a mortgage payment for a laid-off co-worker, God will bring opportunities before us when He wants us to give. Because missional giving is accompanied by joy, genuine opportunities are not seen as excessive, but as ongoing interactions with God. Mark Batterson warns about missed opportunities, "Who might be stuck in poverty, stuck in ignorance, stuck in pain if you're not there to help free them?"[126]

Missional giving is centered in the gospel[127]

The result of the obedience on the part of the Corinthians is that these saints "will glorify God because of your submission flowing from your confession of the gospel of Christ, and the generosity of your contribution for them and for others" (2 Cor. 9:13; ESV). This giving was a direct result of the Corinthian believers' relationship to the gospel of Christ. The power of the Good News led to their confession of its truth and obedience to it. This obedience to the gospel displayed itself in generosity to give in the period of trial.

Missional giving is always centered in the gospel. Anyone who claims to be a follower of Christ, yet is not obedient in the area of giving is not gospel centered; they may not even be gospel oriented. It is clear that not every disciple develops into Christlikeness at the same rate or along the same line; however, no one is a fully devoted follower of Christ until he or she is discipled into missional giving. While Paul did not command them in the specifics about this offering, he desired the Corinthians to "excel" in the grace of giving in the same way they had in other areas.

To be gospel centered is to demonstrate radically realigned priorities based on the person, work, and working of Jesus Christ. As we have seen, the worship of possessions cuts directly to the heart of what it means to be a follower of Christ. We are yet guilty of worshiping mammon if in this area we remain or become radically misaligned.

In the parable of the sower (or soils),[128] seed is distributed onto four types of landscape. The seed is portrayed as the Word, which has in its nature to bear fruit. Some of the seed is thrown on the pathway around and in the planting area, some lands in rocky soil and some on good soil. Some seed lands in a fourth area, "among thorns," where, as explained by Jesus, "the cares of this world, the deceitfulness of riches, and the desires for other things entering in choke the Word, and it becomes unfruitful."[129] The application to missional giving is that materialism works against the gospel, so much so that a person who formerly bore fruit can cease doing so if the Word becomes choked out by cares of this world, love for wealth, and desires for stuff.

If it were only that easy

It would be great if we would just read a few verses, convert to being missionary managers, and commence with our missional giving. In truth, some will do so more quickly than others. Working against all of us, though, in addition to our own conflicting desires, the evil one has any number of temptations in his employ. Attention needs to be given to some of the enemies we will face as we pursue missional giving.

meditations

Using the following space, reflect on what Scripture impacted you the most in this chapter. What response does God require of you?

chapter seven

enemies of missional giving

"Do not covet...anything that belongs to your neighbor."
Exodus 20:17 (HCSB)

"I've worked hard and I've become rich and friendless and mean. In
America, that's about as far as you can go."
Horace Vandergelder (Walter Matthau)
Hello Dolly!

The person who puts his or her trust in things is as great a fool as the
person who denies the existence of God altogether.

Periodically when I was a kid, my family would visit my Granny and Paw Paw in Clanton, Alabama. They lived in a wooden house, well-shaded by several enormous oak and pecan trees across the yard and near an old barn and smoke house where Granny stored her jellies, preserves, and canned vegetables. The front yard had a slight slope toward a hill that angled further down to the dirt driveway that led from Enterprise Road up to their house. It was there that my cousins and I played King of the Hill.

King of the Hill is typically a boy's game—a rough-and-tumble human version of young bucks butting antlers or mountain goats clashing horns. The objective was to remove the cousin or cousins standing at the top of the grade by whatever means necessary and send them sprawling to a place topographically less prominent. Sometimes the dethroning was the result of a one-on-one engagement—hand-to-hand combat, if you will; sometimes it was the mutual effort of a hastily made alliance. Such an alliance was never formalized; rather, it amounted to two people grabbing each arm of the current king and dragging him down. The alliance then was immediately broken as the usurpers turned on each other for final control. For a brief and shining moment, one boy could flex his scarecrow-thin arms at the rest and declare himself, "King of the hill!" That reign would last until the fallen gathered themselves, raced back up the incline, laid hands on the grassy monarch and pitched him unceremoniously forward to less lordly surroundings.

All in all it reminds me of Washington, D.C. Or Wall Street.

The battle for generosity is like a spiritualized version of King of the Hill. We must actively dethrone all enemies, as often as is necessary, and submit our hearts, minds and possessions to Jesus Christ for His use and for His glory. In the New Testament, Paul once pictured this dethroning as caging anti-God thought processes so they could not retain control. He wrote to Christ's followers in Corinth, "We destroy arguments and every lofty opinion raised against the knowledge of God, and take every thought captive to obey Christ" (2 Cor. 10:5; ESV).

As we previously considered, Jesus posits materialism (mammon) against God for control of our lives. It is to one of these two masters that each person has the opportunity to yield. The yielding takes place as we decide how we will relate to our possessions, since we cannot be wrongly related to our possessions and rightly related to God. Jesus emphasized that we *cannot* serve God and mammon; to love and serve one means hatred and despising of the other. The Scriptures point to a number of sins that hinder the follower of Christ from missional giving.

That's what I want

One of the more well-known stories in the Bible is related to covetousness and involves a businessman farmer.[130] This particular farmer had a record harvest, so abundant he would not be able to store it in his barns. At this point he had a number of options. He could have sought out those in need and blessed them with unexpected food. He could have thrown a "Harvest Party" for the town where he lived, giving glory to God for this unexpected blessing.

He might have sought the wisdom of the town's elders in the event there was an issue about which he was unaware, but with which he could help by selling some grain and using the proceeds to address the problem.

Instead, his decision was to demolish his existing barns and build bigger barns in order to store his grain and his goods. Then he would relax and, as we might say, "live off the interest for the rest of his life." In true hedonistic style, he phrased it, "Relax, eat, drink, be merry."

He could very well have been a 1990's dot-com investor if we did not know any better.

His decision warns us of some dangers associated with

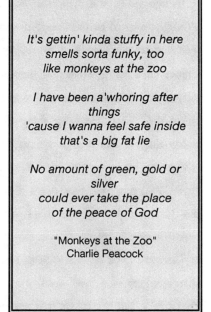

It's gettin' kinda stuffy in here smells sorta funky, too like monkeys at the zoo

I have been a'whoring after things 'cause I wanna feel safe inside that's a big fat lie

No amount of green, gold or silver could ever take the place of the peace of God

"Monkeys at the Zoo"
Charlie Peacock

covetousness and greed. First, the man was already rich. This was not an issue of some schlub winning the grain lottery, going from the poorhouse to the penthouse, from so low to the silo. We are not told how his wealth was accrued, but it is not too far a stretch to figure he had been a successful farmer. His decision to build bigger barns for storage was an outcrop on a life already established on *keeping* rather than *giving*.

Also, he did not see his possessions in the light of God's ownership. Listen to his language: "my crops," "my barns," "my grain," and "my goods." Nowhere in the story did the man give thanks to God, praise Him for abundant provision, or acknowledge God as creator, sustainer, and provider. A true materialist infected with *stuffitis*, he took credit for every decision and every success.

Additionally, this rich man was foolish about the future. Out of either ignorance or hardheartedness, he presumed upon a future that was not to be. Unwilling or unable to admit that his life was like a vapor, here for a while and then gone,[131] his life was forfeited that very night. Most grievous of all was that he missed everlasting blessing, since the most damaging thing about living under the control of materialism is that it provides nothing in eternity. This side of forever is the only place we will find any usefulness for our toys, trinkets, and trash. You may see someone's iPod or favorite jeans in their casket, but those items will be there unused until they disintegrate. The contrast of this man's life was the very example given to the believers at Corinth, "We do not look at the things which are seen, but at the things which are not seen. For the things which are seen are temporary, but the things that are not seen are eternal" (2 Cor. 4:18; NKJV).

Jesus' story about the farmer ended with a clear warning about materialism. Just like this foolish rich man, "so is the one who lays up treasure for himself and is not rich toward God."[132] The phrase "lay up treasure" in the original language of the New Testament is *thesaurizo*,[133] and is used similarly in Matthew 6:19, where Jesus says, "Do not lay up for yourself treasures on earth" (NKJV). Laying up treasure *per se* is not the problem; the issue, like in real estate, is location, location, location. Foolish people "treasurize" their earthly things, heaping them up like King Tut's tomb and leave them behind in the exact same way. Wise people make treasure out of heavenly things, accumulating them for a future reward.

The setting from which Jesus told the story of the foolish farmer involved a man who was, apparently, dissatisfied with his inheritance. Or, more properly, he was dissatisfied with what his brother was doing with *his* share of the inheritance. Well, what was really going on was that the brother who did not get an inheritance wanted some money, land or chariots from the brother who did get the inheritance and, in first-century *People's Court* style, wanted Jesus to make a ruling. Jesus, who was not about to be whipsawed in this brotherly beatdown, responded, "Man, who made me a judge or arbitrator over you?" (Luke 12:14; ESV). It was then that the Lord drilled down to the real issue, which was not about who was getting what when Dad died, but the condition of the son's heart that made him so concerned about the stuff that would be left behind. "Take care, and be on your guard against all covetousness," Jesus told the man, "for one's life does not consist in the abundance of his possessions" (v. 15; ESV).

The money pit: debt

Not only is covetousness a potential king of our heart's hill that needs to be brought low, the accumulation of excessive amounts of debt is also an enemy to missional giving. One popular financial advisor encourages getting out of debt as a means of "financial freedom" so we can have "the money to do God's will in our lives."[134] While the idea may be disputed that doing God's will *always* entails something to do with money, there can be little dispute that the kind of sacrificial, missional giving that should be the norm among God's people is often hindered by excessive debt. The late Larry Burkett wrote, "We have enough money in North America to fund all the Christian work in the world if the people would just give. Unfortunately, money needed for ministering to others is often tied up in large monthly payments."[135] Jerry Rankin concurs, "When we live beyond our means, we reveal that our priorities and values are not biblical but worldly and materialistic."[136]

> *The gold and glitter*
> *towering wonder*
> *it's all within the walls of*
> *Babylon*
>
> *Strength and security*
> *comfort and safety*
> *what could be better*
> *than living in*
> *Babylon?*
>
> *But their strength was*
> *just an illusion*
> *now this city lies*
> *in broken ruins.*
>
> "Bye, Bye, Babylon"
> Whiteheart

Our recent worldwide economic downturn has affected both believers and non-believers. For many, the problem was little savings and much debt; they were so far upside down that they could not even stand on their head to see the top. As a result, believers and non-believers alike have lost leveraged possessions and filed bankruptcy.[137] Henri Nouwen's thoughts on giving space to God include a word study of *absurd* and *obedient*. This comparison provides a tremendous insight on our time when Christ's followers listen to mammon more than God,

We have often become deaf, unable to know when God calls us and unable to understand in which direction God calls us. Thus our lives have become absurd. In the word 'absurd' we find the Latin word *surdus*, which means 'deaf.'

"A spiritual life requires discipline because we need to learn to listen to God, who constantly speaks but whom we seldom hear. When, however, we learn to listen, our lives become obedient lives. The word 'obedient' comes from the Latin word *audire*, which means 'listening.'[138]

When Jesus said, "A student is not above his teacher, but everyone who is fully trained will be like his teacher,"[139] it was both a sign and a warning. The wrong teacher inevitably yields a disciple (a learner) with the wrong focus. Nouwen's diagnosis is that we have not listened closely enough to God and are, therefore, disobedient. The flip side is that we have listened closely to mammon and have followed it into full obedience.

Which way did it go, George?

A third enemy to missional giving is a lack of planning. Paul's encouragement to the Corinthians was to prepare an offering for which they had already planned.[140] Missional giving does not flow from a distracted heart or a lackadaisical mind. Missional giving does not just happen; it comes from a passion for God and God's mission. It is **the** priority item in our budgeting; it is **the** reason for possessions God has put under our management. We should plan both to give and how we will give. While I agree with the spiritual theme of Donald Whitney's statement, "How we use money for ourselves, for others, and especially for the sake of God's Kingdom is from first to last a spiritual issue,"[141] I think he, perhaps inadvertently, creates a false trichotomy. All is under God's kingdom; it is not a third issue added to self and others. We need to have a plan as to how our giving impacts the kingdom of God, under which umbrella lies *everything* having to do with our lives on this earth.

This planning is nothing less than determining how the King wants His funds, currently under our management, invested in or dispersed throughout His kingdom. As we plan according to Kingdom priorities,

When you're hiding underground the rain can't get you wet

But do you think your righteousness could pay the interest on your debt?

I have my doubts about it

"City With No Children"
Arcade Fire

we trust that God can and will sufficiently guide us as His Word promises.[142] What we find is that when we plan to give, we give; without a plan to give, giving becomes more sporadic with many opportunities squandered.

What's number one?

Closely related to a lack of planning is a lack of discipline. This deficiency can both keep us from planning and from sticking with the plans we have developed through prayer and listening to God. (The road to hell being paved with good intentions and all that.) Even some who plan to give fall through with the implementation; it's as if they packed for a long trip and left the GPS or wallet on the kitchen table. There will always be plenty of distractions to keep us from remembering to give. Randy Alcorn writes, "It's this hit-and-miss approach to giving that Paul wished the Corinthians to avoid: 'On the first day of the week, each one of you should set aside a sum of money in keeping with his income'" (1 Cor. 16:2; NIV).[143]

A number of years ago, we developed the habit of writing the checks that represented our giving first after being paid each week; in other words, we wrote the check to our local church, then our mission support checks, then the bills. We did this for two reasons: first, so that we would not forget and find ourselves rushing around on Sunday morning to get it done or forgetting altogether. Second, we did it so we did not watch the "balance" column in our check register get lower and lower before writing the most important checks. This one decision helped build needed discipline in our management practices. The exercise of discipline in our giving helps us to not fall prey to the distractions in what Swindoll calls, "[our] cluttered, complicated world."[144]

A ministry position I once held included working with the benevolence team. Occasionally, when those wanting money called our church office, I would field the initial contacts. I remember a specific lady who called because they needed to pay a bill. In the course of the conversation, she revealed that they attended our church regularly. That was rather a surprise to me, so I asked, "Do you and your husband tithe regularly?" "Yes," she said. "All the time." I was shocked, so I asked, "You mean to tell me that you and your husband regularly give 10 percent of your income and you cannot afford to pay this bill?" She responded, "That's right. Each week I write out the bills that are due, like the cable, rent, phone, or groceries, *then we give 10 percent of whatever we have left*." Even if you believe that tithing on your net income is a biblical position, they had taken it to the extreme! Because they had never disciplined themselves to give of the "first fruits,"[145] they were giving God the stems, cores, and peelings, with predictable financial problems as the result. Their lack of discipline may also have been tied to the next enemy: a lack of faith.

Hey, God, I trust You...kind of

Missional giving depends upon faith in God's willingness and ability to provide for our needs. It takes seriously the admonition not to worry about tomorrow, trusting God for today since today has enough trouble of its own. After giving, it trusts that God is able to stretch what we have leftover in a supernatural way, or supplement it in a providential way. Missional giving recognizes that on occasion our finances may not make much sense on paper, but they make sense in God's economy.

When I was a teenager and young man, my family was acquainted with a single mother in our church, Brenda, and her two children. Brenda wrote a monthly article for our church's newsletter chronicling her walk with God; it was a mix of humor and truth enjoyed by a lot of people. I remember one article in which Brenda wrote of God's unfailing provision, even mentioning a box of detergent, like the widow's jar, that continued to fill the scoop long after it should have been fully used. Her son, Jay, now a pastor, wrote how he remembered,

"going to the candlelight service on Christmas Eve every year at our church. When we would get back to our car, there would always be presents for the whole family. It was good stuff we needed like clothes. My mom may have found out before she died but at the time we only had guesses who was doing that for us. I still don't have a clue.

"I can think of two people from our church that gave her their car. I think she paid a dollar for one and made a gallon of sweet tea for the other one. We always had *car* problems but we never had car *problems*. No matter what hose blew or belt snapped, there seemed to always be another free car waiting in the wings."[146]

Brenda's faith was rewarded by God' provision, though she never attained any appreciable level of wealth.

"Without faith it is impossible to please God."[147] There is no biblical reason to think that faith is necessary in all areas of life except finances. Faith is necessary for this life and the next. It makes no sense that people can claim to trust God for eternal life, but struggle to trust Him for daily bread.

Can tithing become sinful?

Many people reading this book have been taught "tithing;" that is, giving 10 percent of their income through the ministry of their local church. If you are one of those, have you ever considered the possibility of tithing becoming sinful? No, that is not an excuse to quit doing it; it is a challenge not to get stuck at 10 percent. Let me explain.

I was taught to tithe from my youngest days, so I tithed whenever I earned money cutting grass, raking leaves, or on the funds from whatever odd job found me. When, as a senior in high school, my first actual job arrived, I tithed without hesitation; I thought it was just the right thing to do. When Sonya and I married, we continued to tithe faithfully; it was assumed, not discussed. Eventually, though, we came to realize that it took absolutely no faith at all to write those tithe checks. God had long

> *God money's not looking for the cure*
>
> *God money's not concerned about the sick among the pure*
>
> *God money let's go dancing on the backs of the bruised*
>
> *God money's not one to choose*
>
> *Head like a hole*
>
> *Black as your soul*
>
> *I'd rather die than give you control*
>
> "Head Like a Hole"
> Nine Inch Nails

since proven Himself faithful to meet our needs, so we never spent one second wondering about it. We were being obedient, was not that the sum of what He wanted from us?

The issue became this: our giving no longer required faith. We were not giving beyond our ability. For many years we had factored tithing into our finances and had simply learned to live without that money. In a very real sense, God never had to show up at all in our finances; our giving never required His intervention and it never required any measure of faith. This situation developed despite the Bible's teaching, "Whatever is not from faith is sin."[148] If we learn anything from the "Great Faith Chapter," Hebrews 11, it is that faith is always inextricably linked to an outward expression of it. Abel was not commended simply for his faith, but for the obedient offering that resulted from his faith (v. 4); Abraham was commended for leaving his homeland without map, GPS or AAA membership (v. 8, 9); Sarah for trusting God for birthing a child when she could have been a great-grandmother (v. 11), and so on. All believers are thus admonished, "Without faith it is impossible to please God."[149]

In the same way, our faith in God's ability to provide for our needs is expressed not simply in verbal affirmations, but through obedience in our managerial responsibilities. We give when God says give, we give how much God says give, and we give to whom God says give. It is His; we are merely the channels of Him carrying out His business.

In one of the churches I have served, I had a sweet widow serve for a while as my ministry assistant. She was a thoroughly genuine follower of Christ who had a passion for God's mission. On an occasion when we were just sharing some things about life and the

Lord, she told me how, when her husband was alive, they had increased their Kingdom giving until it had reached 50 percent of his income.[150] When her husband died in a hunting accident, she received the proceeds from life insurance. She said, "I knew that God wanted me to demonstrate faith and invest 50 percent in His kingdom, the same amount we had been giving." Her investment was leading a team to an Eastern European country, armed with hundreds or thousands of Bibles to distribute while ministering to children in orphanages. She footed the entire expense herself.

When God gives the opportunity for us to give, in effect He is merely moving assets from one part of His kingdom to another. Or, as we might think of it, from one account to another. If God moves money from my possession for the purpose of meeting a need somewhere else, I can have faith that God can move assets from another account back under my management whenever I have a need to cover. This idea was expressed to the Corinthians like this: "You should give now while you have a personal abundance, so the abundance of another might help you when you need it."[151]

But I just need a little more

Another usurper king to be dethroned is discontentment. A good biblical definition of contentment is "satisfaction in God regardless of my possessions, status or situation."[152] From our earliest days, those of us in the West are bombarded with advertising. Television, radio, billboards, newspaper, Internet, magazines, and smart phones all portray what could be if we were cool enough, rich enough, shrewd enough, or good looking enough. The battle for contentment begins as early in our lives as any other struggle we will ever endure. Our Lord says, "Don't worry about your life," but we grab for every promise of extending youthfulness. He says, "Don't worry about what you'll wear," but JC Penney, Aeropostale, and Eddie Bauer are calling. And we can handle it when He tells us, "Don't worry about tomorrow," because we have TD Ameritrade, right?

By the time we are adults, the default position for contentment involves many more possessions than the Bible declares are necessary. Paul told Timothy, "If we have food and clothing we will be content with these" (1 Tim. 6:8; HCSB). How badly does that fly in the face of our modern or postmodern expectations? Having been saturated with a 'health and wealth' understanding of the gospel or the belief that a sign of God's blessing on America is our financial prosperity, how many American believers could possibly be content only with something to eat and something to wear? I do not know if I could.

Is having only food and clothes God's expectation for everyone? Probably not, although Jesus Himself drew attention to His lack of earthly housing,[153] and the writer of the New Testament book of Hebrews held in high esteem those who "wandered in deserts and mountains, in dens and caves of the earth" (Heb. 11:38; NKJV). Somehow I do not think he was referring to Cro-Magnon Man. These were believers, our brothers and sisters in Christ who "wandered about in sheepskins and goatskins, being destitute, afflicted, tormented" (Heb. 11:37; NKJV). The fact they were listed with others, who were mauled by lions, lends to the idea that homelessness was the exception not the rule.

Paul did not equate contentment with being poor or rich, but assured the believers in the Roman colony of Philippi that contentment was possible whether in abundance or poverty.[154] This happiness with what he had was only possible because Paul had not elevated his stuff into the realm of personal treasure. His influence on believers from the first century down to our day is evidence that he was entrusted with the true riches of which Jesus spoke.[155]

Ah, who cares?

The final enemy to missional giving that we need to consider is a lack of compassion. David Phillips argues that *emotion* leads to *thought* which leads to *action*.[156] Moses was rescued because the daughter of Pharaoh had compassion on him,[157] the mother whose child was threatened by King Solomon saw the baby's life spared because of her compassion,[158] God's promise to return Israel back to their homeland was based on His compassion,[159] and many of Jesus' healings were motivated by compassion.[160]

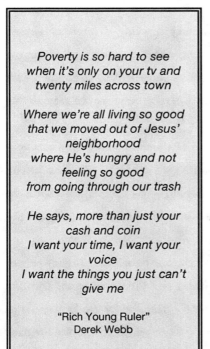

*Poverty is so hard to see
when it's only on your tv and
twenty miles across town*

*Where we're all living so good
that we moved out of Jesus'
neighborhood
where He's hungry and not
feeling so good
from going through our trash*

*He says, more than just your
cash and coin
I want your time, I want your
voice
I want the things you just can't
give me*

"Rich Young Ruler"
Derek Webb

The result is if we lack compassion toward those in need, it is less likely that we will give to meet that need. Just think about it: if you are a political conservative, when is the last time you gave to Greenpeace? If you are a political liberal, when is the last time you sent money to the NRA? If you are a

Christian, when is the last time you sent money to Islamic Relief? The lack of giving cannot be solely attributed to philosophical differences. We do not give because we have no empathy; we are not compassionate toward them, therefore it does not figure into our giving plan, therefore we do not give. (This is not advocacy for donation to Greenpeace, the NRA, or Islamic Relief or other specific charity; these are used merely to show the role of compassion in giving.)

There is a reason, you know, why starving children or abused animals are shown on those fundraising ads. If the organization can tug on the appropriate heartstrings, we may be motivated to give, whereas a bunch of cold statistics on a dark background rarely secures the same result.

Compassion is the central theme of a well-known New Testament story. The story of the good Samaritan, an unnamed man who helped a stranger—the victim of a mugging—has come to represent compassion even for those not familiar with the Gospels (think of the references to a "good samaritan who stopped to help with the accident" on the local news). Two religious people had already passed by this wounded man without offering any assistance at all. The one who did help was from a race generally despised by the Jews of Jesus' day, yet was held up as the example from which to learn. Christians today must be compassionate lest we fulfill the observation noted by Carl F.H. Henry in the middle of the last century. Using the story of the good Samaritan as a backdrop, he wrote, "Fundamentalism is the modern priest and Levite, by-passing suffering humanity."[161]

Obedience defeats the enemy and the enemies

These hindrances to missional giving (our enemies as well as our enemy, Satan) can be overcome via simple obedience. Paul told us that all the thoughts we have that work against our knowledge of God are to be brought into obedience to Christ. Temptations to do wrong are not obligations to do wrong; a tempting thought does not necessitate a follow through. Jesus died to release us from that kind of bondage, giving us both the freedom and will to live obediently to Him.

Missional giving, as practiced by the missionary manager, allows us to join God in His mission in this world experiencing immeasurable blessings along the way. Then, in eternity, we find that, as with all things springing from the grace of God, the reward far outweighs the sacrifice.

meditations

Using the following space, reflect on what Scripture impacted you the most in this chapter. What response does God require of you?

part three

the eschatology of missional giving

or

how does this deal end, exactly?

"Well done, good and faithful servant."
Jesus Christ

"The LORD knows the days of the upright, and their inheritance shall
be forever."
Psalm 37:18 (NKJV)

He is no fool who gives what he cannot keep
to gain what he cannot lose.
Jim Elliott

chapter eight

faith's treasure

"He who overcomes shall inherit all things, and I will be his God and
he shall be My son."
Revelation 21:7 (NKJV)

"Then the King will say to those on His right, 'Come, you who are
blessed by My Father, inherit the kingdom prepared for you from the
foundation of the world.'"
Matthew 25:34 (HCSB)

Too many of God's children live as if their only inheritance is on earth
and miss the chance to add to their inheritance in heaven.

Charlene de Carvalho-Heineken inherited some money. Charlene inherited a **lot** of money. Her father, Alfred Heineken, who died in 2003, left her a fortune of more than seven billion dollars, made from Holland's premium beer which bears his name.[162] No matter what you think of beer, seven billion dollars is a lot of suds.

The three sons of Ingvar Kamprad stand to inherit a pretty large amount of money, too. They sit on the board of IKEA, the furniture company founded by Kamprad, who is their father. If things go as they hope, each will inherit billions of dollars.[163] That is an awful lot of flat-boxed furniture.

The four heirs to Sam Walton's fortune, built through the success of the Wal-Mart chain, each inherited billions of dollars at their father's death in 1992. By 2004, his widow and their four children were worth an estimated twenty billion dollars each.[164] That is a significant amount of groceries and clothes (and tools and tires and...).

Abigail Johnson's family controls 49 percent of Fidelity Investments, the largest mutual fund company in America. In 2009, she was worth around 11.5 billion dollars.[165] Even though mutual funding has not been kind to her of late it looks as if she has still enough shares to support herself.

Numbers like these can boggle the mind of a person who has wealth, and stagger the mind of the average person striving to make ends meet on forty thousand dollars a year. This kind of money gives rise to comments like, "I'd like to have that for just one day!" I admit, it sounds fun to me, too.

An inheritance that lasts

As it currently stands, most of the people on the planet are not going to have multiple billions of dollars handed over to them in some lawyer's office a week after the death of one or both parents (or that "rich uncle" you have heard about). For those who follow Christ, however, there is an inheritance that awaits that will never shrink in size, is not subject to decay, and cannot be hit with "death taxes" no matter who occupies the Oval Office or is the majority party on Capitol Hill. It is this latter inheritance that stays in the mind, heart, and planning of the missional giver.

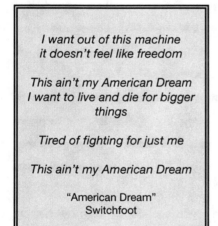

*I want out of this machine
it doesn't feel like freedom*

*This ain't my American Dream
I want to live and die for bigger
things*

Tired of fighting for just me

This ain't my American Dream

"American Dream"
Switchfoot

The apostle Peter explained this inheritance to some early followers of Christ in this way, "Blessed be the God and Father of our Lord Jesus Christ, who according to His great mercy has caused us to be born again to a living hope through the resurrection of Jesus Christ from the dead, to obtain an inheritance which is imperishable and undefiled and will not fade away, reserved in heaven for you," (1 Pet. 1:3, 4; NASB). The same word is used as Paul was speaking in Acts 20:32, "I commend you to God and to the word of His grace, which is able to build you up and give you an inheritance among all those who are sanctified" (NKJV). In Ephesians, this inheritance is guaranteed by the Holy Spirit,[166] is called "glorious,"[167] and is associated with the "kingdom of Christ and God."[168] When Paul encouraged the Colossian believers to serve wholeheartedly as if God was being served rather than man, he spurred them on with this reminder: "knowing that you will receive the reward of an inheritance from the Lord."[169]

In addition to the presence of the Holy Spirit as a guarantee of our heavenly inheritance, the resurrection of Jesus Christ provides assurance, as well. The author of the letter to the Hebrews explains: "Therefore He is the mediator of a new covenant, so that those who are called might receive the promise of the eternal inheritance, because a death has taken place for redemption from the transgressions committed under the first covenant" (9:15; HCSB). How did Jesus become the mediator if He died? Because He was raised from the dead. The Scripture continues, "Where a will exists, the death of the testator must be established. For a will is valid only when people die, since it is never in force while the testator is living" (v. 16). So what we have is this: An inheritance in Jesus Christ was established for all those who would be saved. This inheritance is eternal, reserved in heaven, cannot be corrupted, ruined, or stolen. The inheritance, however, could not go into effect until the person to whom it belonged died; after all, as we know, a will only goes into effect after the death of the testator. So, Jesus Christ died to guarantee the promises of the inheritance, then rose from the dead to become the executor of His own estate! Now, the Bible says the children of God are joint heirs with Christ,[170] which means everything that belongs to Christ belongs to us. We have the same inheritance:

"For all things are yours: whether Paul or Apollos or Cephas, or the world or life or death, or things present or things to come-all are yours" (1 Cor. 3:21, 22; NKJV).

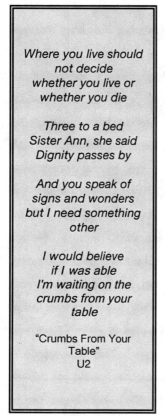

Where you live should not decide whether you live or whether you die

Three to a bed Sister Ann, she said Dignity passes by

And you speak of signs and wonders but I need something other

I would believe if I was able I'm waiting on the crumbs from your table

"Crumbs From Your Table"
U2

Apples and oranges

Let us not mistake this inheritance as if we are trading earthly "stuff" for heavenly "stuff." There does not seem to be any kind of ratio explaining how keeping a smaller less expensive car gets a more prominent mansion in the sky or shopping at a less expensive clothing store translates to an angelic robe from Hart, Schaeffner and Marx. Realistically, the inheritance God offers is freedom from sin, the fruit of the Spirit, Christ-likeness, adoption, abundant life AND eternal life, joy in the presence of God, responsibility, "learning, activity, artistic expression, exploration, discovery, camaraderie, and service."[171] The Bible says that all good and perfect gifts are from God[172] and that He gives us these things richly to enjoy.[173] Joy is found not in hoping for heavenly "stuff," but in knowing the God in whom eternal life is found.[174] Paul, then, could say, "[We are] as poor, yet making many rich; as having nothing, and yet possessing all things."[175]

Our eternal inheritance is a reason why missional giving should be crucially importance to us. The total of all the inheritances in the history of the world pales in comparison to just one share of the inheritance in Christ's kingdom. There is nothing earthly that cannot be corrupted, defiled, stolen, or destroyed. Great works of art can burn, Faberge eggs can be stolen, stocks can lose worth, money can be devalued and fortunes lost. On the other side, the "least" in the Kingdom of heaven is greater than these. When we pay greater attention to temporal, earthly treasures we lose focus on our eternal, heavenly inheritance. A person who dies without Christ to spend eternity in the lake of fire would give Bill Gates's entire fortune for one moment's relief, while a person who inherits the kingdom of God would not trade all the gold ever mined for his or her eternal gain.

Laying them up

This truth about our inheritance expands upon these words of Jesus from the Sermon on the Mount. "Do not store up for yourselves treasures on earth, where moth and rust destroy, and where thieves break in and steal. But store up your yourselves treasures in heaven, where neither moth nor rust destroys, and where thieves do not break in or steal; for where your treasure is, there your heart will be also" (Matt. 6:19-21; NASB). The same eternal security of our inheritance is promised by Jesus regarding our heavenly treasure. I believe the two are related; the treasure is a portion of our inheritance, the portion that we send ahead—by virtue of missionary management of the possessions God puts in our care. It is the principle and interest on our spiritual investment. As we are rightly related to God and to our stuff, treasures are stored in heaven rather than on earth, filling them with eternal significance and imbuing them with eternal security.

The idea of adding to our eternal reward is thoroughly biblical. Paul informed the believers at Philippi that their material obedience was not merely for his benefit, but also for "the profit which increases to your account."[176] Luke records the words of Jesus to the same effect: "When you give a banquet, invite the poor, the crippled, the lame, the blind and you will be blessed. Although they cannot repay you, you will be repaid at the resurrection of the righteous" (14:13, 14; NIV).

The preference of an eternal reward over a temporal reward, as it relates to giving, is also clear from Scripture. Jesus said, "And if you lend to those from whom you expect repayment, what credit is that to you? Even 'sinners' lend to 'sinners,' expecting to be repaid in full. But love your enemies, do good to them, and lend to them without expecting to get anything back. Then your reward will be great, and you will be sons of the Most High, because he is kind to the ungrateful and wicked. Be merciful, just as your Father is merciful."[177] A number of years ago, I worked for a company delivering overnight packages in Atlanta, Georgia. My job required me to spend many hours on sidewalks pushing a hand-truck or carrying small envelopes by hand. As is the case in many urban areas, I was constantly approached by people wanting money. And, strange as it may seem, most of them wanted to go to Birmingham by Greyhound bus; never Macon, Columbus, or Charlotte, always Birmingham.

When I first began to be confronted with those situations, I considered how to talk my way out of it without actually lying. Even though this was many years before debit cards became popular, I

---

rarely carried cash, so most of the time it was not an issue. When I said, "I don't have any money," it was the truth. But on those rare occasions when I was carrying money, I would modify it like this, "I don't have any money *I can give you.*" It was technically true (I could not give it to them since I had other plans for it), but I would use vocal inflections that made it sound more like I had no money at all. On other occasions when I had money and did not feel like arguing, I would usually reach for my right front pocket, where I carried my change and give some coins to the person in need. Then, I would always preach him a short sermonette about how this was really God's money and they should spend it in a way that would please Him. I have always doubted the impact of such a sermon on a drunken man looking for "money for a ticket to Birmingham."

Once, while working a late shift, I was sitting in the far left lane of a one-way street, preparing to turn left. It was a lazy, warm evening and I had the window down. I could see this fellow staggering toward my van like he was following the invisible blade of sidewalk sized pinking shears. He finally made it over to my van and slurred with great gusto: "Hey man, can I have a dollar? I'm not gonna lie to you; I'm a drunk and I wanna get something to drink." What can I say? I gave the man a dollar for being honest and told him as much. Then, for some reason, he started spilling this story of how he had lost his family and ended up on the street an alcoholic. It was brief, since the light changed shortly thereafter, but I've never forgotten it. Giving him a dollar might not have changed him, but it sure changed me.

It was the words of Jesus that led me to give to this man expecting nothing in return. I never expected to get a letter from him with a buck tucked inside, nor did I. And, though I still do not carry cash very often, I have been freed from the need to vouch for how every gift will be spent since a different kind of reward awaits. Slowly I've come to appreciate the words of G.K. Chesterton: "I happen to think the whole modern attitude toward beggars is entirely heathen and inhuman...Everyone would expect to have to help a man to save his life in a shipwreck; why not a man who has suffered a shipwreck of his life?"[178] This is not to say that the mere giving of money is always the best thing to do, but it is to say it is not always the worst.

No explanation

Among the dusty streets of Cairo, Egypt, is a cemetery for American missionaries. Amidst the aging headstones is one for William Borden, a Yale graduate and heir to the Borden family fortune. In 1904 as a sixteen-year old high school graduate, his parents gave him a trip around the world including travels through Asia, the Middle East, and Europe. This trip brought him into contact with many of the world's hurting peoples and birthed in his heart a desire to be a missionary. After graduating from Yale and Princeton, he committed to go to the Kansu, a Muslim people group in China. Before reaching China, however, he stopped in Egypt to learn Arabic. It was in Egypt that Borden contracted spinal meningitis, and within a month was dead at the age of twenty-five.

News of William Whiting Borden's death was carried by most major American newspapers. A biographer wrote, "A wave of sorrow went round the world...Borden not only gave (away) his wealth, but himself, in a way so joyous and natural that it (seemed) a privilege rather than a sacrifice." His gravestone reads, "Apart from faith in Christ, there is no explanation for such a life."[179]

My prayer is that American Christians would passionately embrace our roles as missionary managers and become missional givers. Far from leaving us barren, the rewards are eternal. "Fear not, little flock; for it is your Father's good pleasure to give you the kingdom."[180]

meditations

Using the following space, reflect on what Scripture impacted you the most in this chapter. What response does God require of you?

chapter nine

Christmas every day

"And this is the testimony: that God has given us eternal life, and this
life is in His Son."
1 John 5:11 (NKJV)

"Thanks be to God for His unspeakable gift."
2 Corinthians 9:15 (KJV)

"For God so loved the world that He gave." Thus begins the most well-known, most oft-quoted verse in the entire Bible.[181] No exploration of giving, even an introductory one, would be complete without mulling over what it meant for God to give. It probably is not too great a stretch to label God the first missional giver, if His giving is measured by His love and by the cost. He loved enough to give His Son to save those who were unlovely, unloving, and unlovable. If, in the course of reading this book, you have come to realize the empty, vain nature of trusting things, and, if you are thinking that Jesus is your only hope for eternity, this chapter was written with you in mind.

Giving was at the center of God's plan in eternity before there was a need for a plan in time. The Bible says that Jesus was the Lamb slain from the foundation of the world.[182] We not only find in Scripture that it was God's pleasure to give the Kingdom to His children, but also for Him to give Jesus, so the adoption of

> *Let me ask you one question*
>
> *Is your money that good?*
>
> *Will it buy you forgiveness?*
>
> *Do you think that it could?*
>
> *I think you will find*
>
> *When death takes its toll*
>
> *All the money you made*
>
> *Will never buy back your soul*
>
> "Masters of War"
> Bob Dylan

those children could be possible.[183] The letter to the Romans demonstrates that all things God gives us are the result of the sacrificial death of Christ: "He who did not spare His own Son, but delivered Him up for us all, how shall He not with Him also freely give us all things?"[184] There is no blessing, which God originally intended for humanity, that we have not received (or will not receive) in Jesus Christ.

The agnus dei

Yet, consideration of the depth of the Father's gift would be incomplete if we did not think about how great the sacrifice Jesus Himself made. It was He who left the majesties and glories of heaven in coming to earth. He set aside His rights, retaining both His divinity and His Sonship, and lived for thirty-three years in the likeness of humanity. He lived among the sinful, yet was without sin. He experienced hurt, fatigue, abandonment, and betrayal. It was He who gave up His own life; not allowing anyone to take it from Him,[185] He yielded Himself up for our forgiveness. The Father gave His Son and the Son gave Himself. The selfless and sacrificial giving that made redemption possible is the pattern that informs our own missional giving. It may sound like a cliché, but we truly are never more like God than when we give for the purpose of displaying His glory.

Scripture says in 2 Corinthians, "For you know the grace of our Lord Jesus Christ, that though he was rich, yet for your sakes he became poor, so that you through his poverty might become rich" (8:9; NIV). The poverty attributed to Christ is the same word as the Macedonian's poverty described earlier in the passage. Jesus left His Father's side, He left His throne, He left His glory. He indeed stepped into poverty that we might experience His riches. Each divinity-dishonoring act that Jesus humbly endured contributed to the perfection of His sacrifice; a sacrifice on my behalf and yours. Each temptation He overcame further defeated the power of Satan—whose power was ultimately destroyed at the cross—allowing us to live in freedom from the fear of death and the bondage of sin. His faithful obedience to the commandments of God released me from the curse of a law I could never keep.

None of this would be possible—freedom from sin and condemnation, eternal life, reconciliation to God, salvation—had God not first *given*. This is the joy of the gospel: you and I can be brought into a harmonious relationship with God by the indescribable gift *of* God.

Setting things to rights

It does not take an intellectual giant to discern that things are problematic in this world. Something is rotten and it is not only in Denmark. Even a cursory glance of news headlines reveals murder, rape, child abuse, environmental disaster, economic abuse, genocide, financial collapse, and on it goes every single day. Only the most hopeful of optimists (may I say "insanely hopeful"?) could think

> *(Hey) I'm the king of things I've always despised*
>
> *I'm the gingerbread man*
> *who got eaten alive*
>
> *I'm half baked!*
> *I'm fake!*
>
> *But see I've got hotels on*
> *Park Place and Boardwalk*
>
> *And two hundred bucks*
> *I pass go but, oh!*
> *Life's taken its toll*
>
> *Have I won monopoly to forfeit my soul?*
>
> "Company Car"
> Switchfoot

that things are on some type of upward trajectory. Even within the heart of the hardest skeptic beats the idea that somehow this world is way off track (in fact, this very argument is often used to dispute God's existence). Yet, only with the Good News of Jesus Christ do we find the transformative power of God in the midst of all this calamity.

It is through Jesus Christ that our dead spirits are brought back to life, it is through Jesus Christ that the spiritually poor are made rich, that the wayward become children, that enemies are turned into friends, that hell is exchanged for heaven, that vanity is traded for hope, insecurity for peace, hate for love, and fear for power. Receiving Jesus Christ is the biggest no-brainer in the history of no-brainers. Our salvation would be utterly impossible were it not for the gift of Jesus Christ; utterly impossible, except that with God all things are possible.

Jesus Christ is indeed the only way to be reconciled to the God of creation. The claim of His own mouth is "No one comes to the Father except through Me." This is no small thing; in fact, it is the biggest thing in the time and eternity. Jesus sets Himself up as the only gateway to eternal life, the only way to a full life here and the only way to know the One who made us.

The scripture says, "For by grace you are saved through *faith*, and this is not from yourselves; it is God's gift-not from works, so that no one can boast" (Eph. 2:8, 9; HCSB). Faith, is not only necessary for our financial obedience, but for entering God's family initially. The rich young man we saw in chapter three rejected Christ, not because he was ignorant of what lie *ahead*, but because of what lie *between*. He would have known heaven was ahead of him, but he would not live without his stuff between his encounter with Christ and his eternal reward. He missed the certainty of treasures in heaven because of the uncertainty of following Christ. But, God can be trusted! And He can be trusted for both time and eternity.

The gift of eternal life is just that: a gift. Early believers in Rome received this truth, "The wages of sin is death, but the gift of God is eternal life through Jesus Christ our Lord."[186] Eternal life is not earned by what we do for God; it is received because of what Jesus did for us. If, as you read this book, it became clear that you do not have eternal life, and if you are willing to turn from your sins and receive Jesus Christ, you can be reconciled to God, become a co-heir with Christ, and a participant in God's mission. It is to this end that I pray.

meditations

Using the following space, reflect on what Scripture impacted you the most in this chapter. What response does God require of you?

appendix

holier than thou:
is poverty more spiritual than wealth?

One of the most admired Christians since the ascension of Christ must be Giovanni de Pietro de Bernardone. He was born in the twelfth century, at a time when the dominant church in Europe was Roman Catholic. The son of a wealthy businessman who stood to receive a large inheritance, Giovanni was nonetheless restless and, like many modern warriors, longed to be a knight. Being a knight in feudal Europe was a little like being a plastic surgeon in Hollywood: no lack of opportunity to ply the trade. Unfortunately for Giovanni, style did not win out over substance, and his top-of-the-line knightly apparel was not enough to prevent his capture during his first crusade. Subsequent imprisonment saw him languish for a year waiting for Daddy to pay his ransom.

A second foray into battle ended when he had a vision of God speaking to him. The Catholic Church during this time was embroiled in as many scandals as had ever plagued it. One writer explained, "The church was hemorrhaging credibility; it was seen as hypocritical, untrustworthy, and irrelevant. Some people even wondered if it would survive. Clergy were at the center of all kinds of sexual scandals. It had commercialized Jesus, selling pardons, ecclesiastical offices, and relics...Popular songs ridiculing the church and clergy could be heard all over Europe...The church had also become dangerously entangled in the world of power-politics and war."[187] Upon returning home, Giovanni went to a dilapidated chapel in San Damiano. It was quite literally falling apart with its walls cracked and roof caved in. While praying, he heard a voice telling him, "Go and repair My house. You see it is falling down."

Convinced he had heard from God, the young heir began raising funds to repair the chapel. He stole valuable fabric from his rich, merchant father, selling it (and Dad's horse) to help pay for the chapel reconstruction. When his father found out, he was understandably furious and brought his son before the local bishop to be punished for his thieving ways. The entire town turned out to see what would happen to the young man. In the midst of his tirade before the bishop, Giovanni's father turned to see that his thieving son had quietly stripped off all his clothes and was standing stark naked and alone.

Giovanni walked over to his father, placing all his clothes at his feet along with the money he had received for selling the cloth and the horse. He said, "Until today, I always have called Pietro di Barnadone my father. From this day forward, I have only one father, my Father in heaven." So moved was the bishop that he, with the town of Assisi looking on, draped his own robe around the young St. Francis, walking him away from his old life and into the new.[188]

Each time I read the story of St. Francis of Assisi I am struck by the depth of his repentance in the showdown with his father. While I'm not a defender of all he taught and did (and I'm not looking to go hear any nude preachers anytime soon), Francis' clear obedience to Matthew 10:37 always rattles my teeth. And, I'm not alone. St. Francis remains the hero of many, not the least of these was one of my heroes, the late Rich Mullins.

The life of Francis, who renounced his wealth and position, the life

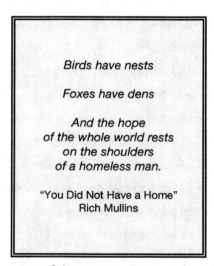

Birds have nests

Foxes have dens

*And the hope
of the whole world rests
on the shoulders
of a homeless man.*

"You Did Not Have a Home"
Rich Mullins

of a woman like Mother Teresa among the lepers of Calcutta—like anyone who has ever chosen a vow of poverty begs the question: Is a life of poverty to be desired? Is it intrinsically more holy than being prosperous?

Though there are warnings to the wealthy and though the poor are known for not having many of the same anxieties as the rich, the Scripture does not seem to indicate that being poor is holier than affluence, nor that it is necessarily more desirable. When the prodigal son had wasted all his money on a sin-saturated binge, he was left in a miserable state of poverty, but this state of affairs was not better than his wealthy father who waited expectantly for his return. In fact, it was as much poverty of soul as of finances that led him to repentance. The Bible says that people do not despise a man who steals bread to eat when he is hungry, yet warns that, if caught, he will still be found guilty under the law.[189] It also warns that poor people may be deserted by their friends,[190] were not to be shown any favoritism in legal matters,[191] can be victims of destruction,[192] and can be dishonored even in church.[193] Various rabbis taught that being poor was worse than all the plagues on Egypt put together, worse than all other miseries and the worst affliction a human could experience.[194] And a sweeping study commissioned by the World Bank found that those in low-income countries describe themselves with words like, "shame," "humiliation," "garbage," "unhappy," "inferior," and "helpless."[195]

The poor are also not immune from covetousness. The same sin that vexes the wealthy—causing them to live for *more* stuff—can vex the poor, wanting to live for *some* stuff. Materialism does not require an abundance of materials to be the object of worship. In his highly regarded book, *The Spirit of the Disciplines*, Dallas Willard makes this observation, "The percentage of those in bondage to wealth is no greater among the rich than among the poor. It is not money or gain, but *the love of it*, that is said by Paul to be the root of all evil (1 Tim. 6:10), and none love it more desperately and unrealistically than those without it"(emphasis in original).[196]

There are in the world today those who choose to be less well off, intentionally shunning a better class of living, often for the purpose of reaching the poor who might otherwise be marginalized or ignored. In Manila, The Philippines, there is a gigantic garbage dump named "Payatas" which is so large that people actually live at the edges in shanties (some actually in the dumps) and sustain their existence as scavengers amid the refuse.[197] A typhoon in 2000 precipitated the collapse of a seven-story pile of rubbish at one of these dumps killing more than two hundred people.[198] I once read of a missionary who owned almost nothing, living on the trash pile leading a church for the squatters and scavengers.

While on a learning trip to Campo Grande, Brazil, I met another man who was poor for the sake of the gospel. I first noticed this "hippie" sitting on the steps of the church beside a little display of necklaces, bracelets, and earrings he had made from wire, thread, and beads. As we entered the building, the pastor of the church nodded back toward him and said, "You see that hippie? He's a member of our church!" I later found out that he received Christ while living the carefree hippie life. At the time of my trip, "the hippie" was planning to attend Bible college so he would be better prepared to reach those in the hippie subculture; however, he was not planning to leave it. He said, "If I don't stay and reach 'my people,' who will?" Instead of cutting his hair, getting a better paying job, and getting on a church staff somewhere, he chose poverty as the means of reaching other hippies.

These and others provide living answers to John Stott's musing, "Should we not continue to simplify our own economic lifestyle, not because we imagine that this will solve the problem, but because it will enable us personally to share more and to express appropriately our sense of compassionate solidarity with the poor?"[199]

Thankfully (for those with wealth), Kingdom influence is not limited to the poor. I am familiar with a man, wealthy in real estate, who has given hundreds of thousands of dollars to mission work over just the last few years. The foundation started from Christian businessman Arthur S. DeMoss' estate has given away millions over the years. Christian millionaire and missional giver, R.G. LeTourneau, gave away

90 percent of what he made to Kingdom and philanthropic causes and lived on the remaining 10 percent. Jesus did not say it was impossible for a rich person to enter the Kingdom of heaven, only that it was difficult.

The very fact that both Old and New Testaments have so much direction about helping the poor assumes that there will be some people who are able to do it! If everyone were poor, who would help the poor? There is an expectation in Scripture that some people will have wealth; they are not castigated for such, only warned against its dangers and encouraged toward righteous use of it. Stott reminds us that Jesus does not preclude possessions, savings, or even wealth. "What Jesus forbids is the selfish accumulation of goods; extravagant and luxurious living; the hardheartedness which does not feel the colossal need of the world's underprivileged people; the foolish fantasy that a person's life consists in the abundance of his possessions; and the materialism which tethers our hearts to the earth."[200]

Poverty is not more holy than wealth, and it is not necessarily more to be desired. There are advantages and disadvantages to each position. If the poverty is neither due to laziness nor the wealth due to greed or unethical business practices, the follower of Christ can be assured that God can be glorified by holy living in either situation.

meditations

Using the following space, reflect on what Scripture impacted you the most in this chapter. What response does God require of you?

conversations

This section is to help stimulate spiritual growth by encouraging reflection, discussion and further learning based on the subject matter in *The Generous Soul*. Conversation starters can be used in small group Bible studies sponsored by a church, a work group or home group; the format also lends itself to Sunday School class use. There is no direct connection between the individual chapters of the book; this is by design so that the group can utilize this resource to best meet its needs. It is not necessary to follow in order questions I through 20. The numbers are provided primarily for points of reference. The discussion can follow any flow that creates the best response and growth opportunity.

___

I. Marty wrote about giving away some things to friends at church. What are some things that you might give away to someone who would appreciate it? Once you have identified the gift and the recipient, how quickly can you get it to them? What will you say to let them know of God's leading in your decision to give?

2. Do you struggle with the idea of God owning everything? How will you reconcile any doubts with what God's word teaches?

3. Read these verses from the Old Testament (Genesis 1:1, Psalm 89:11, Isaiah 40:12-15) and these verses from the New Testament (John 1:1-3, Colossians 1:16). Think about which one speaks most powerfully to you about God's creative power. Why does it impact you in such a way?

4. Think of something that you made either as a child, teenager or adult that you ultimately gave away. It could have been a craft in Vacation Bible School, a project at Boys Scouts, a gift for a parent or something for a friend's home. As the creator of it, how did you decide to whom you would give it? Did the emotional connection you had with the item affect your decision to give? How?

5. Now think of someone distributing items for a Thanksgiving benevolence drive to help the poor or Christmas boxes going out of the country. Under normal circumstances is there an emotional tie to those items? How does the difference between this and #4 help us see our role as managers rather than owners?

6. In the famous O. Henry short story, *The Gift of the Magi*, a cash strapped young couple desperately wants to purchase each other gifts at Christmas. She, unbeknownst to her husband, sells her most valuable possession, her long hair, to buy him a fob chain for his pocket watch. He, also in secret, sells his beloved pocket watch to

purchase jeweled combs for her hair. Have you ever had to sell anything meaningful out of need? How did the emotions involved affect the decision? How should it change our response to accept that God is merely moving His assets around when we are in those circumstances?

7. Perhaps the fact that most people never leave their home culture supplies a reason we do not immediately think of ourselves as missionaries. What are some concrete steps you might take to make this perception about your own life become more biblical?

8. If the worship of mammon betrays itself by our emotional bond with our stuff, what does that say about who (or what) you worship? Why is it so easy for us to make a distinction between materialism and idolatry?

9. The way we change objects of our worship is by repentance, turning from one way of doing things to another. In this context of this book, it would be a change to God's way of viewing money and possessions. How might a person demonstrate repentance from worshiping things (see Luke 3:7-14)?

10. Write down the name of some people in your circle of influence who have yet to receive the gift of salvation and pray for them now either individually or in your group.

11. Almost everyone wants to spend eternity with God, yet often we treat our finances as if there is no God at all. What can you do this week to demonstrate that God is Lord of your finances?

12. How would you define generosity in relationship to our being missionary managers? Marty confessed to struggling with being "generous by degrees." Do you find this same struggle to be true in your giving opportunities?

13. In your current giving practices, how do you respond when opportunities to give are presented to you? How do you decide when to give and when not to give?

14. Think about a time when God provided for you (or your family) either through a miracle or through His providence. If you are alone right now, take time to write it out and give thanks to God again for it. If you are in a group, share an instance or two about God's specific provision.

15. Read Matthew 16:1-12. In this passage, Jesus warned the disciples about the dangerous teaching of the scribes and Pharisees. However, because they had forgotten to bring bread on the trip, the disciples thought Jesus was concerned about what they were going to eat. He reminded them of two separate miracles of provision. Do you ever find it hard to trust God to provide even when He has already demonstrated His faithfulness in your life? Why?

16. Have you ever had to say "no" to any expenditure due to your financial support of God's kingdom work? If "yes," did you ever consider the inheritance you were laying up in heaven? If "no," what will it take for you to prioritize God's kingdom over mammon?

17. In a society that urges us to "have what you want," how can you learn to be content, or "want what you have"?

18. God is a giver; He loves to give good gifts to His children. Giving is a part of who He is. When we give, we are living like our Father and cooperating in work with Him. Does looking at it from this perspective stir up any feelings or thoughts?

19. Pick a certain time of year (Thanksgiving or Christmas, for example) to financially bless a ministry or an individual. Involve the entire family in contributing to this offering and in making the decision on who receives the blessing. What are some things you can do to increase the offering amount (skip going out to eat once a week, having a yard sale, limiting family Christmas gifts)? How will you remember that you are being a channel through which God is moving His assets around?

20. If you have children what are some steps you can take to help ensure that they mature with a biblical view of money and possessions?

endnotes

introduction
1. http://www.answerbag.com/q_view/1760516, accessed July 26, 2010
2. Driscoll, Mark and Breshears Gerry. *Doctrine: What Christians Should Believe.* (Wheaton, IL: Crossway, 2010), 374.
3. Swindoll, Charles R. and Zuck, Roy B. *Understanding Christian Theology.* (Nashville, TN: Thomas Nelson Publishers, 2003), 898.
4. Brady, Diane and Palmeri, Christopher. "The Pet Economy," http://www.businessweek.com/magazine/content/07_32/b4045001.htm, accessed July 28, 2010
5. Ibid.
6. http://thewaterproject.org/digging-wells-in-africa-and-india-how-it-works.asp, accessed July 28, 2010
7. The Neuticles website states that more than $229,750,000 been spent on Neuticles through July 2010.

part I section page
8. Merrill, Eugene. *Everlasting Dominion: A Theology of the Old Testament.* (Nashville, TN: Broadman and Holman Publishers, 2006),130.

chapter one
9. Tozer, A.W. *The Pursuit of God.* (Camp Hill, PA: Christian Publications, 1993), 22.
10. "Homes Lost to Foreclosure On Track For 1M in 2010," http://www.cbsnews.com/stories/2010/07/15/ap/business/main6679691.shtml?tag=mncol;lst;2, accessed July 28, 2010.
11. Hemphill, Ken. *Making Change: A Transformational Guide to Christian Money Management.* (Nashville, TN: Broadman and Holman, 2006), 3.
12. Psalm 14:1 for instance.
13. The point of this paragraph is not to argue over how God created the universe, i.e., Day-Age, Seven Day, or Gap theories. I only want to establish that if God did not create the universe, He has no ownership claim to it. If He did create it, by whatever method He chose, then He is owner.
14. Allen, Paddy. 'Monster star': R126a1 compared to our solar system," http://www.guardian.co.uk/science/interactive/2010/jul/21/monster-star-r136a1-sun-planets, accessed July 29, 2010.
15. Psalm 50:10
16. Haggai 2:8
17. Quoted in Kelly, J.N.D. *Early Christian Doctrines.* (Peabody, MA: Hendrickson Publishers, 2004), 86.
18. Deuteronomy 8:16-18, NASB. While this reminder is clearly given to Israel as a sustained promise made to Abraham, Isaac and Jacob, even the strictest

Dispensationalist must admit God's blessing of the power and wisdom to create wealth is true regarding even believing Gentiles in the Church Age. If not, we have a situation in which humanity has become wealth *creators* and, therefore, have an ownership claim to stake. This would be in contradiction to the clear tenor of the scriptural whole.

19. Blaise Pascal. *Penses* (Krailsheimer, A.J., trans.) (New York, NY: Penguin Books, 1966,) 179.
20. http://www3.telus.net/st_simons/nsnews019.html See also, http://en.wikipedia.org/wiki/R._G._LeTourneau , http://www.letu.edu/about_LU/museum/Museum_Online/index.html, all accessed August 13, 2010.
21. Matthew 18:23-35
22. Luke 16:1-8
23. Matthew 21:28-32
24. Matthew 24:42-51, Mark 13:34-37, Luke 12:35-48
25. Matthew 25:14-30, Luke 19:12-27
26. Matthew 5:3
27. Tozer, A.W., *The Pursuit of God*, 23.

chapter two
28. Luther, Martin. *The Works of Luther*, quoted in Geisler, Norman. *Systematic Theology, Vol. Two.* (Minneapolis, MN: Bethany House, 2003), 531. *Emphasis mine.* Scripture quote John 5:17, ESV.
29. Oden, Thomas C. *The Living Word.* (Peabody, MA: Prince Press, 2001), 287, 288.
30. Strong, Augustus H. *Systematic Theology.* (Valley Forge, PA: Judson Press, 1906), 410, 411.
31. Merrill, Eugene. *Everlasting Dominion: A Theology of the Old Testament,* 129. *Emphasis mine.*
32. Que Sera, Sera (Whatever Will Be, Will Be) was written by Jay Livingston and Ray Evans. It was first performed by Doris Day in Alfred Hitchcock's *The Man Who Knew Too Much* (1956).
33. "But our God is in the heavens; He does whatever He pleases." Psalm 115:3 (NASB)
34. See I Kings 18.
35. See Exodus 14.
36. Joshua 10:12, 13
37. 2 Kings 19:32-37
38. John 6:1-14

chapter three
39. Dickens, Charles. *A Christmas Carol, The Chimes and Crickets on the Hearth.* (New York, NY: Barnes and Noble Classics, 2004), 70.
40. Ibid, 71.
41. http://en.wikipedia.org/wiki/Hetty_Green, accessed July 26, 2010.

42. Keller, Tim. *Counterfeit Gods.* (New York, NY: Dutton, 2009), 51.
43. Nee, Watchman. *Love Not The World.* (Wheaton, IL: Tyndale House, and Fort Washington, PA: Christian Literature Crusade, 1978), 71.
44. Groeshel, Craig. *The Christian Atheist.* (Grand Rapids, MI: Zondervan, 2010), 180.
45. Ibid, 181
46. Psalm 115:4-8
47. Colossians 3:5
48. This John R.W. Stott quote came from my sermon notes, which were not footnoted. The original source is unknown to me.
49. http://www.bing.com/Dictionary/search?q=define+materialism&FORM=DTPDI A, accessed August 10, 2010.
50. http://atheism.about.com/od/philosophyschoolssystems/p/materialism.htm, accessed August 10, 2010
51. http://www.bing.com/Dictionary/search?q=naturalism&go=&form=QB, accessed August 10, 2010.
52. Brown, Harold O. J. *The Sensate Culture.* (Dallas, TX: Word Publishing, 1996), 9.
53. Ibid, 10
54. Grudem, Wayne. *Systematic Theology.* (Grand Rapids, MI: Zondervan Publishing, 2000), 267.
55. See Romans 1:22-25
56. This phrase is a play on the chorus of "The Stand," written by Joel Houston, recorded by Hillsong United. Full lyrics can be found at http://artists.letssingit.com/artist-j3gh2sb, accessed Aug 7, 2010.
57. Hagopian, D., Demar, G., and Karchmer, J. (Producers), & Doane, D. (Director). (2009). *Collision: Christopher Hitchens vs Douglas Wilson* [Documentary-DVD]. United States: Crux Pictures/Gorilla Poet.
58. Luke 18:18-25
59. See the Appendix, *Holier Than Thou: Is poverty more spiritual than wealth?*
60. Levitt, Steven D. and Dubner, Stephen J., *Freakonomics.* (New York, NY: William Morrow, 2006), 11. *Emphasis in original.*
61. Mark 10:28
62. "How The Average U. S. Consumer Spends Their Paycheck," eds. http://www.visualeconomics.com/how-the-average-us-consumer-spends-their-paycheck/, accessed July 28, 2010
63. *Giving USA*, a publication of Giving USA Foundation™, researched and written by the Center on Philanthropy at Indiana University (2009).
64. Piper, John. *Future Grace.* (Sisters, OR: Multnomah Books, 1998), 324.
65. I do not have the original source of this quote, but found it here: http://www.lifeprinciples.net/SuccessatLife.html, accessed August 5, 2010.
66. See Ephesians 5 and James 4:3, 4
67. Bonhoeffer, Dietrich. *The Cost of Discipleship*, Rev. Ed. (New York, NY: Macmillian Publishing, 1975), 318

68. Tozer, A.W., *The Pursuit of God*, 22. *Emphasis mine*.

part two section page
69. Nee, Watchman. *A Table in the Wilderness*. (Wheaton, IL: Tyndale House Publishers, and Fort Washington, PA: Christian Literature Crusade, 1987), July 4 devotional (no page number).

chapter four
70. Any of these biographies are recommended reading. The story of the Huaorani people's engagements with the gospel can be read in *Through Gates of Splendor*, by Elizabeth Elliot and watched in the movie, *The End of the Spear*.
71. Matthew 28:18-20. See also, Mark 16:15, Luke 24:46-49, John 20:21, Acts 1:8
72. John 20:21
73. John 1:6
74. In his book *Exiles* (Hendrickson Publishers, 2006), Michael Frost uses the similar phrase, "host empire."
75. Rankin, Jerry. *Spiritual Warfare*. (Nashville, TN: Broadman & Holman, 2010), 98.
76. Ibid, 100, 101.
77. Luke 12:48, author's paraphrase.
78. "To satisfy the world's sanitation and food requirements would cost only US$13B, about what the people of the United States and the EU spend on perfume each year." http://library.thinkquest.org/C002291/high/present/stats.htm, accessed August 17, 2010.
79. Colossians 3:2, NKJV
80. Matthew 6:19, NKJV
81. 2 Corinthians 5:20, ESV
82. Matthew 6:34, ESV
83. Klein, Maury. *The Change Makers*. (New York, NY: Macmillan, 2004), 57.
84. Adapted from Matthew 25:14-30 and Luke 19:12-27
85. Luke 16:10-12
86. 1 Corinthians. 4:2
87. Edersheim, Alfred. *The Life and Times of Jesus the Messiah, Vol. 2*. (New York, NY: Longmans, Greene and Co., 1907), 460.
88. McLaren, Brian, Sweet, Len and Haselmayer, Jerry. *A is for Abductive: The Language of the Emerging Church*. (Grand Rapids, MI: Zondervan, 2003), 107.

chapter five
89. Mark 12:41ff, Luke 21:1-4
90. Edersheim, *The Life and Times of Jesus the Messiah*, 388.
91. Alcorn, *Money, Possessions and Eternity*. (Carol Stream, IL: Tyndale House Publishers, 2003), 6, 7.
92. Isaiah 9:17, 10:2, Jeremiah 49:11, Zechariah 7:10, Malachi 3:5

93. You really should do some research on this, but be prepared for a shock. The name seems to purposefully obscure the obscenity of their worship. I don't recommend an in depth discussion about it in the Middle School Boys Sunday School class.

94. http://www.biblemap.org/#Sidon, http://www.biblemap.org/#Zarephath, both accessed August 1, 2010. This event is used by Jesus in Luke 4:26 as an example of God's kingdom expanding beyond the Jews, where were rejecting it, to the Gentiles, who would receive God's word as the Sidonian widow did.

95. 1 Kings 17:12, ESV

96. 1 Kings 17:14, ESV

97. http://www.biblestudytools.com/commentaries/matthew-henry-complete/1-kings/17.html, accessed August 1, 2010.

98. http://library.thinkquest.org/C002291/high/present/stats.htm., accessed August 4, 2010. An estimated 30 million people died in the Great Famine of China between 1958-1961while 750k-1.5M people died in the Irish Potato Famine of 1845-1851.

99. 1 Kings 17:17ff

100. I modified the phrase "with a whirlwind to fuel my chariot of fire" from Rich Mullins' song, *Elijah*.

101. Nelson, David P., *A Theology for the Church* (Danny Akin, ed.). (Nashville, TN: Broadman & Holman, 2007), 268.

102. Cumbers, Frank, ed. *Daily Readings from W. E. Sangster*. (Westwood, NJ: Fleming H. Revell, 1966), 214

103. See 2 Chronicles 16:9

chapter six

104. 2 Corinthians 8:6, 16

105. Cole, Neil. *Church 3.0*. (San Francisco, CA: Josey-Bass, 2010), 248.

106. 2 Corinthians 8:1

107. 2 Corinthians 8:2

108. twitter.com, CSLewisDaily Twitter feed, accessed July 29, 2010.

109. Acts 11:27, 28

110. Blomberg, Craig. *From Pentecost to Patmos*. (Nashville, TN: Broadman & Holman, 2006), 372.

111. 2 Corinthians 8:3

112. 2 Corinthians 8:4, 9:7

113. 2 Corinthians 8:4

114. Blomberg, *From Pentecost to Patmos*, 46.

115. Ibid, 221. Blomberg theorizes that Paul's offering was also about bridging the gap between the Gentile and Jewish believers as about meeting physical needs. He notes, "Scholars have often speculated that Paul placed a special importance on this offering because he hoped to show the more conservative Jewish churches in Israel that the Gentile believers in the Diaspora recognized the debt they owed to the 'mother church.'"

116. 2 Corinthians 8:5

117. 2 Corinthians 8:8, 24
118. Revelation. 3:15, 16
119. I John 2:15, 16
120. 2 Corinthians 9:6
121. Hemphill, *Making Change*, 138.
122. Psalm 112:9 is from the ESV as is 2 Corinthians 9:10
123. 2 Corinthians 9:11, ESV, emphasis mine.
124. 2 Corinthians 9:8
125. Original in my files.
126. Batterson, Mark. *Wild Goose Chase*. (Colorado Springs, CO: Multnomah Books, 2008), 11.
127. 2 Corinthians 9:13
128. Matthew. 13:3-9, Mark 4:3-9, Luke 8:5-8
129. Mark 4:19, NKJV

chapter seven
130. Luke 12:13-21
131. Psalm 39:5, 39:11, 62:9; James 4:14
132. Luke 12:21
133. See also Romans 2:5, I Corinthians 16:2 and 2 Peter 3:7.
134. This concept has been popularized recently by Dave Ramsey.
135. Burkett, Larry. *The Word on Finances*. (Chicago, IL: Moody Press, 1994), 180.
136. Rankin, *Spiritual Warfare*, 86, 87.
137. By the middle of 2009, bankruptcy filings in the U.S. had reached a staggering 6,020 *a day*. http://www.usatoday.com/money/economy/2009-06-03-bankruptcy-filings-unemployment_N.htm, accessed July 29, 2010
For the fiscal year ending June 30, 2010, consumer bankruptcies were up 21 percent over the previous year, http://www.suntimes.com/business/2615694,CST-NWS-BANKRUPT19.article, accessed July 29, 2010.
138. Nouwen, Henri J.M. *The Only Necessary Thing*. (Greer, Wendy Wilson (ed.). (New York, NY: Crossroad Publishing, 1999), 82.
139. Luke 6:40, NIV
140. 2 Corinthians 9:5
141. Whitney, Donald S. *Spiritual Disciplines for the Christian Life*. (Colorado Springs, CO: Navpress, 1991), 133.
142. For instance, Proverbs 16:9, "The heart of man plans his way, but the Lord establishes his steps" (ESV) and Psalm 37:23, "The steps of a *good* man are ordered by the LORD, And He delights in his way." (NKJV).
143. Alcorn, *Money, Possessions and Eternity*, 199.
144. Swindoll, Charles. *Intimacy With The Almighty*. (Dallas, TX: Word Publishing, 1996), 28.
145. Proverbs 3:9, 10
146. Personal correspondence on file.

147. Hebrews 11:6, HCSB

148. Romans 14:23 (NKJV)

149. Hebrews 11:6 (NIV)

150. My memory is that she was not working outside the home during that time, but it may be incorrect. Regardless, he was the primary breadwinner.

151. 2 Corinthians 8:14, author's paraphrase.

152. I modified this from Merriam-Webster to reflect a biblical perspective.

153. Matthew 8:20

154. Philippians 4:11. Interestingly, the Greek word that Paul uses to describe his 'need,' is *hysteresis*, the same word used in Mark 12:44 to described the poverty of the widow who gave two coins.

155. Luke 16:11

156. Phillips, David. *Holy Rewired: Science, the Gospel, and the Journey Toward Wholeness*. (Smyrna, DE: Missional Press, 2010), 49.

157. Exodus 2:6

158. 1 Kings 3:26

159. Jeremiah 12:15

160. See for instance Matthew 14:14, 15:32, 20:34, Mark 1:41, 5:19, 9:22.

161. Henry, Carl F. H., *The Uneasy Conscience of Modern Fundamentalism*. (Grand Rapids, MI: Wm. B. Eerdmans Co., 1947), 2.

chapter eight

162. http://www.forbes.com/lists/2010/10/billionaires-2010_The-Worlds-Billionaires_Rank.html, accessed August 13, 2010. Carvalho-Heineken's wealth stood at $7B at the time of the Forbes 400 list.

163. Ibid, forbes.com, Forbes 400 list.

164. http://www.pbs.org/newshour/bb/business/wal-mart/sam-walton.html, accessed August 13, 2010.

165. forbes.com, Forbes 400 list.

166. Ephesians 1:14

167. Ephesians 1:18

168. Ephesians 5:5, NKJV

169. Colossians 3:24 (HCSB)

170. Romans 8:17, Galatians 4:1, Hebrews 6:17-20

171. Alcorn, Randy. *The Treasure Principle*. (Sisters, OR: Multnomah Books, 2001), 38.

172. James 1:17

173. 1 Timothy 6:17

174. John 17:3

175. 2 Corinthians 6:10, NKJV

176. Philippians 4:17, NASB

177. Luke 6:34-36, NIV

178. While this is not the original source of this statement from Chesterton, it can be found here: http://francesblogg.blogspot.com/2006/04/what-is-beggar.html

179. Alcorn, *The Treasure Principle*, 36, 37 and "No Reserves. No Retreats. No Regrets. William Borden's Life" http://home.snu.edu/~HCULBERT/regret.htm, accessed August 13, 2010.
180. Luke 12:32, KJV

chapter nine
181. John 3:16
182. Revelation 13:8
183. Romans 8:15
184. Romans 8:32, NKJV
185. John 10:18
186. Romans 6:23, KJV

appendix
187. Cron, Ian Morgan. *Chasing Francis*. (Colorado Springs, CO: Navpress, 2006), 45, 46.
188. This section was adapted from Cron, *Chasing Francis*, 50-52.
189. Proverbs 6:30, 31
190. Proverbs 19:4
191. Leviticus 19:15
192. Proverbs 10:15
193. James 2:2-6
194. Edersheim, *The Life and Times of Jesus the Messiah Vol. 2*, 342, note 2.
195. Corbett, Steve and Fikkert, Brian. *When Helping Hurts*. (Chicago, IL: Moody Publishers, 2009), 52.
196. Willard, Dallas. *The Spirit of the Disciplines*. (New York, NY: HarperCollins Publishers, 1988), 199. The chapter entitled "Is Poverty Spiritual?" is worth the price of the book.
197. http://www.nytimes.com/2006/05/21/world/asia/21iht-city7.1790859.html, accessed August 12, 2010 and http://www.pbase.com/bobbyw/payatas_dump, accessed August 12, 2010
198. http://wasteage.com/mag/waste_death_toll_rises/
199. Stott, John R. W. *The Contemporary Christian*. (Downers Grove, IL: Inter-Varsity Press, 1992), 193.
200. This quote from John R.W. Stott was taken from my sermon notes, which were not footnoted. As a result the original source is unknown to me.

acknowledgements

Father, Jesus and Holy Spirit: without whom I can do nothing; without whom I am nothing.

Sonya: without whom I'm not much. Thank you for sharing life with me through the ups and downs of these 26+ years.

Timothy: for being funny, nutty, helpful and for your quiet faithfulness.

Abigail: for being a source of joy and amazing example of a godly young lady.

Beth and Jacob: for modeling a young marriage built on Jesus. Beth for proofreading and making manuscript suggestions.

Mom and Dad: for being missional givers before the term existed. And for all that food when I was growing up.

Russ Rankin: Editor and friend. Thanks for the phone calls, texts and dm's while in the desert.

Sam Raynor: Cover designer extraordinaire.

The many Facebook friends and Twitter followers who prayed for me once or often during this writing process.

David Phillips: for another opportunity to publish with Missional Press and a chance to share the dream.

Apple Inc., AT&T DSL, CLEAR 4G, Starbucks, Inman Perk and Barnes & Noble without whom this book would have been hand written and much, much shorter.

To all of my pre-reviewers for your time, energy, encouragement and words of commendation.

Brett Moore: who wanted his name in my book "anywhere."

about the author

Marty Duren is a speaker, author, entrepreneur, consultant, disciplemaker and student. For more than 20 years he has pastored local churches in Georgia, planting one an hour south of Atlanta. He

has been married to Sonya for more than 26 years and has three great children and a genuinely appreciated son-in-law. He enjoys reading, writing and hiking. He also runs and bikes, though purely for health reasons--no enjoyment included.

Marty has participated in Kingdom work on each continent (with the exception of Antarctica), conducting conferences and revival meetings and led mission efforts in many contexts.

He is available for worship services, seminars, conferences, church consulting (staff relations, transitional ministry), and pastoral coaching.

Contact: webmaster@martyduren.com

Friend: facebook.com/martyduren

Follow: twitter.com/martyduren

Also by Marty Duren (with Todd Wright)

JOURNEYS:

Transitioning Churches to Relevance

Available now from:

www.amazon.com

www.bn.com

www.missional-press.com

or your local Christian bookstore.

Commendation for JOURNEYS

Lots of people can tell you what to do. Some can do so through research, others through personal observation, and still others through their intuition. In JOURNEYS: Transitioning Churches To Relevance, Marty and Todd take us on a journey and tell us a story—and it is a worthwhile journey and a moving story. Instead of telling you what to do, Marty and Todd tell their journey from religious role playing to personal transformation...and from personal transformation to fresh expressions of mission and ministry in their churches. I found myself engaged and challenged and believe you will as well.
Ed Stetzer, Co-author
Transitional Church

When it comes to writing books about leading transition in the church, there are three types of pastors. There are those who have led change and do not take the time to write about it. There are those who have not led change but write about how to do it anyway. And there are those that have actually done it well and written it down. Todd Wright and Marty Duren are definitely in the right category.

This book rocks! It is the actual story of how they did it - and provides big insights and big ideas. If your church is transition, this is a must read!
Dr. Dan Southerland, Author
Transitioning: Leading Your Church Through Change

Academics have for some time now heralded a warning that the church needs a conversion experience, from corporate to missional. With honest reflection and insight Marty Duren and Todd Wright take us through a journey, not only of the conversion of their churches, but into the transformation of their own lives as well. They clearly demonstrate that the vision of the pastor is critical to the missional future of the church. Theirs is an insightful journey of transition; a book well worth reading.
Ronald W. Johnson, Professor of Mission and Evangelism
McAfee School of Theology, Atlanta, Georgia

JOURNEYS, by Duren and Wright, is a book which will challenge, encourage, and even disturb readers. It is a brutally honest story of the struggle of two young pastors who yearn to see their churches impact culture for the cause of Christ in a way that is truly effective. They desperately wanted to 'be the church that God was calling us to be in our context and in our time.' The struggles that they faced are honestly included. The lessons learned truly point to God's ongoing ministry to His servants.

It is a call to have a Kingdom philosophy of ministry as well as a missional approach to life. I commend this book to you. It is one that will help the next generation as they struggle in a less than easy environment in seeking to reach an increasingly secular culture.
Dr. Frank Page, President
Executive Committee, Southern Baptist Convention

JOURNEYS: Transitioning Churches To Relevance personifies the amazing persistence of God to graciously shape and effectively use us in His ongoing and always relevant work of restoring relationships with the highest order of His creation--people--of every tribe, tongue and nation. From a missionary point of view, it is a joy to learn of American pastors who are doing the same things that they would expect from foreign missionaries, namely to make whatever transitions are necessary in order to, in a culturally relevant way, faithfully communicate the fullness of God's love to the people of the host culture. Consider this book as a compelling, educational and transparent missionary journal of two pastors who have led their congregations to become both local and global missionaries to the current generations of unreached people living in the United States' Southeast and beyond. May their tribe increase!
Jim Capaldo, Outreach Pastor
ChangePoint Church, Anchorage, AK

JOURNEYS is tremendous; it is compelling, inspiring, challenging...all rolled up in one. I literally could not put it down. All of our staff and elders will be expected to read it as we pray through transitions of our own.
Micah Fries, Lead Pastor
Frederick Blvd Church, St. Joseph, MO

LaVergne, TN USA
17 November 2010
205291LV00001B/113/P